Shifts Only Happen Once You Own Your Sh!t

How to make the unconscious conscious and move from victim to creator...

Catherine Plano, Ph.D.

About the Author

Catherine Plano PhD is an internationally acclaimed Entrepreneur and Fortune 500 Mentor, Transformational Mindset Coach and International Keynote Speaker who has dedicated her entire life to helping others transform their own lives and business into greatness.

Catherine possesses the knowledge and resources necessary to make a long-lasting difference in hundreds of thousands of lives to come. With over two decades worth of experience in brain-based leadership and behavioural neurolinguistics—the neural mechanism in the human brain—Catherine helps leaders build stronger and more effective teams. She has accumulated over 30 years of exploring, researching and teaching metaphysics and has received notable certifications issued by prominent organisations from all over the world.

Catherine's purpose is to unlock human potential by raising consciousness and self-awareness for the betterment of all humankind.

Copyright © 2022 by Catherine Plano

Shifts Only Happen Once You Own Your Sh!t
How to make the unconscious conscious and move from victim to creator...

Edited by: Annie Leeman
Proofread by: Andoni Salvador
Cover Design by: Avek Publishing House

Photos by: mirabellart, coreyford, eleaner & valentina

All rights reserved. No part of this publication may be reproduced, distributed, or transmitted in any form or by any means, including photocopying, recording, or other electronic or mechanical methods, without the prior written permission of the publisher, except in the case of brief quotations embodied in critical reviews and certain other non-commercial uses permitted by copyright law.

Although the author and publisher have made every effort to ensure that the information in this book was correct at press time, the author and publisher do not assume and hereby disclaim any liability to any party for any loss, damage, or disruption caused by errors or omissions, whether such errors or omissions result from negligence, accident, or any other cause.

Adherence to all applicable laws and regulations, including international, federal, state, and local governing professional licensing, business practices, advertising, and all other aspects of doing business in the US, Canada or any other jurisdiction is the sole responsibility of the reader and consumer.

Neither the author nor the publisher assumes any responsibility or liability whatsoever on behalf of the consumer or reader of this material. Any perceived slight of any individual or organisation is purely unintentional.

The resources in this book are provided for informational purposes only and should not be used to replace the specialised training and professional judgment of a health care or mental health care professional.

Neither the author nor the publisher can be held responsible for the use of the information provided within this book. Please always consult a trained professional before making any decision regarding the treatment of yourself or others.

For more information, email support@catherineplano.com.au

ISBN: 978-0-6454161-2-1 (Paperback)

ISBN: 978-0-6454161-3-8 (eBook)

Table of Contents

Introduction	ix
1. The Psychology of Triggers...	1
2. Harness the Power of Patterns...	33
3. Honouring Your Own Boundaries...	61
4. Building True Confidence, Impostor Syndrome, Ego and the Fear of Not Being Good Enough...	89
5. Activating Your Intuitive Intelligence...	123
6. Expand Your Consciousness Using Archetypes to Improve Your Understanding of Others...	151
7. Embrace Your Shadow and Heal Your Wounded Self...	179

Dedication

Thank you to my dearest husband who has given me the space to go through my own dark knight of the soul's journey and at times getting lost down the rabbit hole while trying to find my way out of the labyrinth and still be standing by my side during my own awakening.

To my beautiful son, my little ray of sunshine who continuously inspires me to become a better human being. And to my beautiful pooches who shower me with unconditional love, thank you for bringing me so much peace, joy, and harmony.

To my wonderful readers, know that I am with you every step of your journey and I congratulate you for doing the deep work. Life is all about experiences and you were born for this adventure. Have faith and believe in yourself.

Much love, blessings, and gratitude. Namaste.

Catherine Plano

Mwah xxx

Introduction

First and foremost, if you were triggered by the title of this book, you are in the right place. I too was umming and ahhing about the word sh!t. But it made me ask myself: why am I triggered by such a word in the first place? And so, the journey begins, taking us on a deep dive beneath the iceberg, the shadows, and the unconscious mind to find the truth.

The purpose of this book is to take you through a step-by-step process where you can find the ultimate recipe to release yourself from locked patterns that no longer serve you.

I don't know about you, but I have invested quite a chunk of my life looking for that perfect book or methodology to help me get to where I want to go and be the person I want to be. Well, after years of researching, I have refined my discoveries and simplified them so that you can apply them easily in your own life. And I have recorded them in this book, as my gift to you.

Shifts Only Happen Once You Own Your Sh!t gives you a simple (*yet thorough and powerful*) understanding of shadow work. While the topic can be very complex, I've described everything in the most easy-to-understand and impactful ways possible. We are going to unravel all the ways that you can transcend the darker aspects of yourself and how to make the unconscious conscious and move from victim to creator.

I swear that this is a mind-boggling process at the best of times. But when you allow yourself to go through the journey of undoing all the doings of your life, you will feel a sense of freedom like never before.

For so many years, I sought freedom external to myself. It wasn't until I immersed myself in Carl Jung's work that I realised the freedom I was seeking from the external was actually seeking me—but from the inside. Jung's work can be complex to read and digest. However, I found a way to make it easy on the palate by putting it into practice and sharing some real-life stories to bring it all to life.

It all started with these patterns that were appearing over and over in my life. A different day, a different time, a different person, but the same experiences. We all have a choice, but I wasn't aware of that until now. I can choose to be a victim of my life, or I can take ownership, accountability and take responsibility for all that I want to be, do, or have. So, I chose the latter.

I decided that I had to make this decision since, in all these scenarios and situations, the common denominator was moi! And this helped me shift my perspective from victimhood to empowerment. It's so much more liberating when you own your sh!t.

These patterns had themes to them; they had characters to them; blimey, they even had headlines and stories to them! When I realised this, I felt the etheric slap like never before. I realised that I was the narrator of these stories. I was the narrator, director and scriptwriter of this thing called *'my life'*.

I encourage you to have a journal with you before you commence this journey. As things crop up for you, it is of great importance that you capture them while they are fresh in your mind. Otherwise, they will disappear quicker than you can say: *Hurramadingdong*!

This is a word that I made up some years ago, and it has so many meanings to it! But I just love the curiosity that one has when one hears such a word.

Enjoy this adventure into the labyrinth, filled with intricate passageways, a journey to self-discovery – a new chapter in life waiting to be written. A time for wonder, wisdom, and healing. And know this, when your sh!t comes up, it means you are ready to do the deep work. You've got this!

From my heart to yours, embrace and enjoy the journey. This book will act as your guide and companion. May you prosper and expand beyond your wildest dream, dearest one.

Much love and gratitude,

Catherine

MWAH XX

Chapter 1
The Psychology of Triggers...

"Everything that irritates us about others can lead us to an understanding of ourselves" – **Carl Jung**

Isn't that an interesting concept? And if you find any level of resistance to that quote, know that it is 100% correct! Yes, everything that irritates us about others is our shadow because we are constantly projecting our shadow onto others. Not just a little bit. 100% of the time. All the time.

However, we cannot recognise our own shadow, unless we commit to doing the deep work ourselves, going on an exploration, if you will, and searching for it. You don't have to go too far to find it. What we assume is nowhere to be seen can often be sitting right next to us in a hidden nook or valley.

I would like you to remember a time in your life when you were playing with your physical shadow. You might have been a child skipping and running on a sidewalk or playing with your shadow's reflection on a bedroom wall. Or perhaps you and your siblings got creative and made shadow puppets to resemble a rabbit or dog.

At some point in your life, you were very present and aware of your shadow. It might have run alongside you, trailed behind you, or appeared on the path ahead of you. You just accepted that it was your shadow. You knew that if there was light around you—you would always be able to see your physical shadow. You accepted that it was a part of you and thought nothing more of it.

I would like for you to close your eyes and think about this time you invested with your shadow. It may be a little difficult at first but take your time and eventually, the right moment will come to you. Once it arrives, recall the time and place but most importantly how you felt. When you're ready, open your eyes. What did you experience when you brought forward your shadow?

If you felt heightened emotions such as joy, happiness, safety, fun and all those good-feeling vibes or if you felt completely alone, scared, unhappy, lost and maybe not such great feelings. One very important thing to keep in mind moving forward before we deep dive into some of these concepts is that there is no right, no wrong, no good and no bad.

Non-judgment and acceptance are key to moving forward with this book.

Lucky for us human beings, we have been given the gift of the shadow to find out who we truly are!

If you don't deal with your shadow, it will deal with you...

Over the last couple of years, I have done a lot of shadow work. But after opening Pandora's box of my own shadow, I experienced the opposite of what I feared the most; I was able to shift shame into compassion, embarrassment into courage and limitation into freedom.

When I allowed myself to step out of the illusion that my darkness will ultimately take over, the opposite happened. I now can see the world in a different light that I did not know was possible. It was only in the very presence of my shadow that I could discover what I had pushed aside for all these years. If anything, it brought light to my blind spots. Thus, I was able to work with and integrate those parts.

Embracing the shadow allows us to be whole and to be real. We can take back our power, unleash our passions and realise our dreams, no matter how far they currently appear from our daily routine.

The only conclusion that I have for those individuals who steer away from doing the shadow work (*and I am talking about emptying that closet of yours, pulling out all those little things that reside in the deeper part of your unconscious mind*) is that they can no longer blame or point the finger at anyone.

Instead, you must be fully accountable and own absolutely everything that has taken place until now. This, I know, can be scary for some, since it is so much easier to blame your friends, family, work, or life itself.

You may be thinking right now, *"Okay, so what is the shadow in the first place?"*

Everything we experience in our minds is a manifestation of the soul and results from contrast.

You have no experience in the absence of contrast; to have manifestation, you need opposing energies. Thus, the shadow is a human creation. Like everything in life, creating the shadow is a process.

To put it plain and simple in a digestible, palatable way: *the shadow is who you think you are NOT!*

What we can't be with won't let us be...

Our shadow consists of those parts of ourselves that we don't want to see, acknowledge, or accept. It's multifaceted, meaning you can't fix it with just the mind that created it in the first place. It's not linear, and it's not just negative because in the shadow resides untapped talents, gifts, and potential.

Our goal is to integrate our shadow and accept it by bringing more light to it. The kind of light we experience when the sun comes out on a chilly winter morning. Because the shadow aspects are parts that were not accepted and pushed away, they too want to be seen, heard, and valued.

How many of us have ever thought or said something like: *"I would never do that! That's nothing like me?"*

And how many of us have ever heard or said the phrase: *"As above, so below; as within, so without?"*

What about: *"Your perception is your own projection?"*

So, if we take *'as above, so below'* and integrate it with *'perception is projection'* we can then say: *"As inside, so outside."*

What does this mean? Your shadow is always dancing with you; it is there waiting for its turn to play a part in this wonderful cycle called life. Therefore, it is paramount that you are using what is referred to as the Law of Correspondence, as often as possible because that is where you will find that lost treasure chest.

The Law of Correspondence informs us that our outer world is nothing more than a reflection of our inner world. This is an extraordinary principle. If we pay attention, we realise that our current reality is a mirror of what is stirring around inside us.

If our outer reality is unhappy, chaotic, or unfulfilling, these circumstances are a direct result of what is happening *inside* us. If we have low self-esteem, feel bad about ourselves, or constantly feel anger, hatred, or loathing, then our outer world will be a place of frustration and loss, just to show us what we are projecting.

This then becomes a self-perpetuating situation where we feel bad about ourselves, and our outer world is unhappy. The worse the outer world becomes, the worse we then feel about ourselves, which then has a direct impact on our reality.

To escape from this loop or trap, it is critical to shift our paradigm. And if we want to shift our paradigm, then we must start changing the way we think! Nothing in our outer lives can change without first making changes on the inside. Because what we see in others is really what we see in ourselves. It's an inside job!

All transformation is an inside job...

Focusing on changing the external is unsustainable if we haven't done the work to change on the inside. Our reality will continue to evolve so that it reflects our inner beliefs and world.

No matter what, our outer world reflects our inner world in every way, shape, and form. If we desire change in our outer world, we must first change our inner world and our thoughts, beliefs, and attitudes.

The late Wayne Dyer said, *"If you change the way you look at things, the things you look at change."* You see, how it works is quite simple. If you see, think, or feel a certain way about someone, something or somewhere, you will unconsciously act out or show up in that very way because that is the lens you have decided to wear for that day. And guess what? You will keep on getting the same results over and over and again.

The ONLY thing that we have complete control over in our life is the way we think. We cannot affect meaningful and lasting change until we change our thought patterns to focus on what it is we truly desire. So now you can see the importance of understanding the Law of Correspondence to take control of your life! If you want positive change, look inside first.

Remember, we can activate this Law of Correspondence by becoming aware of our recurring patterns. These tendencies and beliefs are often passed down during our imprinting phase. Early in life, we are imprinted upon via family ties, parental programming and experiences that subsequently reside in that deeper part of our subconscious and unconscious minds. However, as we experience more things in life, these old patterns often hold us back or no longer serve us.

We casually accept that humans experience physical and intellectual growth beyond childhood. Yet somehow the same logic isn't applied to emotional growth—it almost sounds ludicrous to think that we expect ourselves to carry the same emotional state that we were given as a child.

Fortunately, as humans, we are gifted with self-awareness and the ability to reflect on our minds and lives. We can make great changes by *consciously* taking action—steps to break unhelpful beliefs and tendencies.

We must address that little voice in our heads. The one that continuously appears while you read this, telling you to resist change because it is uncomfortable and unaccustomed territory. Remind the voice that comfort is familiarity in disguise, whereas change is simply placing us in a more pleasant situation we just aren't familiar with yet.

To help us in this process, we need to have an open mind and heart. Learning about the shadow is so important. It will ultimately help you unveil to yourself who you truly are! The goal is to recognise the shadow (*in yourself and others*) and work towards integrating and embracing the parts of ourselves we barely want to glance at.

What we judge in others is a disowned part of ourselves...

Look at your current reality. You may focus on one aspect of your current reality or several areas, such as your career, relationships, health, financial situation, etc. Ask yourself, *"How are my inner thoughts and attitudes being reflected in my outer world?"*

If there is someone in your life that you don't like, and they display behaviours that just get on your nerves, then ask yourself, *"Where do I do that behaviour in my life but haven't owned it about myself?"*

Keep in mind, with the Law of Correspondence, that it is what you think, feel and experience internally that you project externally. Let me bring it to life with some examples for you.

If you have a strong perfectionistic side where you demand perfection from yourself and you never want to make a mistake, then how you project that is that you may not be forgiving when others make mistakes.

Another example is if you have a very strong inner critic where your internal dialogue is quick to criticise yourself and you are critical of everything that you do. How you may project this is that you will be critical towards others and oppose new ways of thinking or new ideas. A clear example of this in parenting styles is this, as a parent, you may believe that *'tough love'* will allow your child to become your version of success. But the real reason you are critical is that you believe your success is not enough and you want the opposite for your child.

One more example. If you lack self-love and you are constantly finding faults or flaws in everything that you are, being, doing or having. The way you project that is to find faults in those around you—where you are projecting a lack of self-love all around.

So, how does understanding the Law of Correspondence shift our perception of the events that happen on the external, physical level? And how do we stay emotionally stable and wise during chaos?

Hold the mirror up…

When you find yourself having a negative experience, recognise that somewhere in your inner world, there is disharmony. And your outer world is reflecting that back to you. In other words, your mirror image is not of the true self; it is of the damaged self.

Every day, you are being shown the changes that need to be made and the places in your subconscious that need to be healed. When a negative emotion is triggered, it is important to take the time to understand why you are feeling a particular way and how you are reacting.

Once you have this insight, you can apply the opposite. Once you can connect with the discord that is happening in your outer world, you can transform it by applying opposite energy to attract what you believe you are lacking.

Since our energy is always reflected in us, we can transform our negative experiences into positive ones. When you are faced with something negative, it is the quickest way to dissipate that energy and heal your subconscious mind.

- When you are criticised, praise someone.
- When you are hurt, love someone.
- When you are discouraged, encourage someone.
- When you are afraid, reassure someone.

At that moment, you are mastering the ability to heal a wounded part of you by taking back your power.

Understanding the Law of Correspondence is the first step towards taking control of your life. If you want positive change, look inside first, and remember if you don't have any shadows, you are not standing in your light.

If you don't have shadow, you don't have light...

By tuning in, you'll realise that it is so obvious when the shadow emerges or when it is present. Whenever any aspect of the self has been split off—labelled as bad, guilty, shameful, illicit, or wrong—then the shadow gains power. The main ingredients we used in creating the world and our shadow are these lower vibrational frequencies of secrecy, guilt, shame, and blame.

Our outer world is a projection of our inner world; if we are not happy with what is going on in our lives, we have the power to change it. Isn't that wonderful to know? Let that sink in for a minute. Really let it. Skim over all those little things in your life that you beg to be different and know that they can be. At any moment you like, your life can become that joyous event you replay in your head on repeat.

When we judge, we create duality, separation, and struggle if you will, because the shadow keeps us trapped in two ways. It keeps us unconscious (*meaning asleep*) and on autopilot because it is running the show and erupts with incredible power whenever it wants to!

Duality only exists because one is standing on either end—have or having not, gifting or being gifted, receiving, or giving. But these dualities are not too different in the scheme of things. It all depends on your perception. When we are hanging on too tightly to either end, we can create imbalances.

For example, waiting to receive some news may create an imbalance within you. Because when one hangs on too tightly, it slows down the energy. The energy becomes stagnant because it is figuratively being held in one place.

What about if you were to let go of it all and not hold on to either end but let yourself free, what then? One only hangs on to such a thing with bated breath when one has a mindset rooted in scarcity. However, going back to the shadow loses its power when consciousness stops being divided.

Both light and shadow are the dance of love...

For many people, the term '*shadow*' brings up all kinds of negative and dark associations. Shadows are often depicted as mysterious or misunderstood aspects that we have no control over and that presumably want to harm us.

Because of this, it's easy to assume that shadow work is a dark spiritual practice that involves the negative and sinister aspects of our personalities.

The shadow is dark because we are made of both light and dark aspects, but it's an important part of who we are, and we can't be afraid of that part of ourselves, quite the contrary we need to bring it in close and love it, every single part of it.

The shadow was first introduced to the Western world by psychologist Carl Jung. He described it as the suppressed, rejected, denied, disowned and unconscious part of us and our personalities that the ego fails to see, acknowledge, and accept. It is any aspect of our inner world that is not exposed to the light of our consciousness.

As children, we are born whole and complete, but that wholeness is short-lived and throughout particular childhood interactions the shadow is eventually born.

Imagine this. You're a baby resting in your birthplace, snuggling in a soft, cotton blanket. Given that you are in fact a baby, you rely on those around you to live. Fast forward a little and you are now four months old. Your caretaker has been suffering from newborn fatigue and in a moment of weakness, accidentally loses grip and drops you.

Of course, nobody blames you because it is senseless to do so. Everything that you have experienced so far has been because of the caretaker and those close to them—both their competence and incompetence.

You are a sort of mindless, squishy organism entirely dependent and essentially empty—you have no original feelings or experiences. Everything you experience, and feel is based on what has been shown to you. You were once hollow and are now filled, becoming *'whole'* if you will.

But it was never you that made yourself whole—that's what adulthood is for. It is no longer needing someone else to take care of you. Others no longer decide what is good or bad about you or what should be suppressed or rejected. It's all up to you.

Whether *'parental programming'* exists or not depends on your beliefs. We choose our parents to either break the program, live the program, or rewrite the program.

When you react to a projection you become that projection...

Just the other day I was at a chemist and the pharmacist obviously having a bad day decides to address me from a distance and asks *"what do you want?"* No *"hello"* nor *"please"* ... Immediately I thought *'how rude'* and then proceeded to order out loud from across the counter. It was almost as if I was bothering them and in their way of completing their task. Anyway, you can see where this is going ... the moral of the story is that I reacted to their poor behaviour and left the chemist agitated, annoyed and having a serious complaining session in my mind. It was at that very moment that I realised—I reacted to their projection and became their projection.

Let's have another look at how projections can impact us. When we depend on our caregivers for survival, we suppress the aspects that are disapproved, and we exaggerate the aspects that are approved.

For example, imagine a 5-year-old boy who is very much in touch with his feelings. He is sensitive and emotional. And let's say this little boy saw this Batman outfit that he wanted so badly, but his dad didn't have enough money to purchase such an outfit. And thus, this little boy gets mad—he is kicking, screaming, and crying because he wants that costume, and there is no way that he is leaving the shop empty-handed.

Now, let's pretend the dad, embarrassed by such behaviour, in response to the tantrum, yells out, *"Stop crying like a little girl—you're not your younger sister. Be a man!"*

His dad believes crying is bad, and that it's a sign of weakness, so the little boy suppresses his emotions. As a result, the boy pushes this gentle and sensitive side of himself into the shadows and begins *'acting tough'*.

As an adult, he has trouble processing his feelings and will not show his emotions even when it's required. Because of this incident that happened to him as a little boy, he now struggles in his relationships, never allowing himself to be fully seen, heard or present.

Why even mention this scenario? My dearest, as an adult, when you react to a projection, your triggers are firing—on all cylinders, sort of speaking. Due to our long (*and often unconscious*) history of perceptions and interpretations of past experiences and memories, plus all our associated emotions, beliefs, and values, we project who we are onto our partners, friends, family, and the external world. Our internal reality creates our external reality.

It's enough to make your head spin!

Everybody has a public persona...

We, therefore, create personas based on who we think we need to be. In Latin, persona translates to *'mask'*. It is the image we present to the world.

Our persona is the way we show up in a specific context. This context-sensitive mask is influenced by what and who we focus on. Our persona is the way we present ourselves to the world around us because we want these character traits to be seen by others.

Sometimes, our persona can appear as something we are pretending to be rather than who we are meant to be or who we really are. If we are true to ourselves, then our persona should accurately reflect who we truly are. However, in some cases, individuals present false images or a disingenuous persona to fit in or be accepted by others.

No wonder most of us are too afraid to be authentic—we have had a life of pretending to be someone else. Many of us, having worn different masks for an entire lifetime, have forgotten who we truly are.

Perhaps with our family, we have projected a reserved put—together version of ourselves. Conservative achievements such as academic or work accomplishments are shared at the dinner table. However, if we were at the same table with our friends, we may try to hide these achievements altogether to make them feel better. Instead, gossip and other social matters are the preferred topic.

We have more energy when we stop wearing or hiding behind a mask. Pretending can be exhausting. What's more, it takes up *waaaaaay* too much brainpower. In life, we play many roles; we have a multitude of responsibilities and interact with many people.

We can get so lost in the roles we play—and that just leads to stress and confusion. Yes, the closer we remain to who we really are, then the less confusing it becomes.

Let's look at this from a practical point of view. Define when you are playing a *'role'* – for example, corporate career woman, mother, father, sympathetic friend, lover .... Can you pinpoint the particular attributes in the different roles you play? For example, if you are a leader in a large corporate firm you may display more *'confidence'* in comparison to when you are at home with your partner.

We are conditioned—as much as we try not to be—to take on the *'attributes'* we believe these roles should have. But when you get really clear with yourself (*and the difference in you might be really subtle in any given role*) then you can understand *'how'* and *'when'* you play these roles, you can start to merge them a little, so you can step from one role into another... one at a time!

Grab a piece of paper and write down all the roles you have. Now, underneath write how you behave, your needs in this particular role and how often you find yourself in this role. Do you see differences? What are they?

What this means is that for all of us, there is some serious juggling taking place, moving us further away from who we truly are. These roles we play—these personas don't resemble who we truly are.

The ego wants quantity...

Now that we understand what the persona is, let's look at the *'ego'*. Essentially, your ego is who you consciously consider yourself to be. Who are you? What makes you likeable? What are your attributes? What are you known for?

Whatever comes to mind in response to these questions is a part of your ego. It consists of different parts of your identity, such as your name, occupation, relationship status and roles you play in life.

We all have egos. But are you aware of what your ego is sabotaging? It could be sabotaging your relationships or that job opportunity you always wanted.

Having a powerful ego can be hard to admit as most of us associate *'having a big ego'* with being, well, rude or self-centred. But we all have an ego. Ultimately, it's healthier and more realistic to work with the ego's energy rather than deny or fight against it. When we balance ego with soul, we find a happier, less competitive, and more peaceful and loving way of being.

How do you know when it's your ego standing in the way of you and others? This one is super easy to identify, it's when the driver has a very *'external'* focus.

Let's pretend you are at work, and you are with your team, brainstorming and collaborating on a project. Suddenly, one of your team members corrects you in front of everyone. Yep. In front of everyone, no filters.

In their eyes, they may see it as helping you use the correct word or language for this particular project. However, you feel attacked, offended, vexed and even angry, to the point where you shut down and take it as an insult. Now, that's a perfect example of your ego having a problem. It's not you!

When you allow your ego to control your thoughts, feelings, and actions, it creates confusion, deception, and delusion. It can also cause rifts between yourself and others.

Osho an Indian Guru once said, *"The ego is happy when it can take something."* In other words, if you feel that someone is taking something from you, more than likely, your ego has stepped in and taken control.

The ego is an imitation, a romanticised illusion, and an incomplete version of you. It's not your soul's true identity. Nevertheless, it does have its collection of thoughts, feelings, values, and beliefs.

Your ego has developed and accumulated over time to fit in with your community, culture, company, or world around you. Essentially, the ego only has one purpose—to protect you. Yes, I know it sounds contradictory, but it is here to keep you safe from your fears. In saying that, your ego is not your amigo.

And if your ego and persona(s) are out of alignment, your shadow is activated. You are probably thinking *'what the?'* right now, but I promise, you will walk away with a bit more insight.

The ego is what keeps us separate from our truth...

Imagine an iceberg. It is our ego that sits and mediates between the conscious (*the peak of the iceberg*) and the unconscious (*below the surface*). Therefore, it is called the subconscious where our accessible memories and knowledge reside. This part is responsible for reality tastings and a sense of personal identity.

The ego is the conscious part of our personality, the part where our common sense and reason lie. It allows us to organise our thinking and our judgments on the external world. The other side of the iceberg, underneath the deep blue sea, consists of this massive invisible part of our unconscious mind and the collective unconscious. Here, buried in that deeper part of our unconscious mind, is where our shadow dwells.

When we first see our shadow, we jump with fear. It scares the living daylights out of us. We know when our shadow is activated by the way we feel. Whether the emotional hook, pull or charge is positive or negative in nature, it is our shadow waving at us trying to get our attention.

For instance, have you ever looked up to someone and said, *"You are magnificent, you are so amazing at what you do, no wonder you are so successful!"* Well, this is a perfect example that it is your shadow at play here. It is letting you know that you don't own these certain qualities and you must if you want to succeed.

To show how it works both ways, have you ever heard yourself say, *"I would never do that to a person in public!"* Yet again, this is your shadow pointing to something that you don't own as yours.

This doesn't mean that it is that specific event (*content*) taking place in that exact environment (*context*). You would need to chunk it up by saying, *"where in my life do I speak like that and in what context?"* It could be in a business sense, in the way you speak to your loved ones at home, or even something as simple as self-talk.

To get a clearer picture of your own shadow, here are a few questions to ponder over:

- What are some things that I dislike about myself?
- What are some things that I dislike in others?
- What are some things I complain about?
- What are some things I criticise in others?

- What are some things I struggle with?
- What are some things I envy in others?

It is our shadow that challenges our ego. In essence, the ego is not bad. We need the ego. It has a purpose: to mediate between the conscious and the unconscious. Therefore, your relationship with your ego is up to you. It can be your ally or your foe.

Think about it. If we didn't have the ego to intervene and negotiate between the conscious and the unconscious mind, what kind of mess do you think we would end up in? If we didn't have an ego, who would then be the one that would moderate our desires, our appetite, our values, and our beliefs? Our ego helps us create healthy boundaries because it is the 'I' in us.

The shadow grows bigger and bigger as you repress…

When we repress and deny things about ourselves, they do not disappear; quite the contrary, they expand and accumulate power. Over time, this repression and denial cause us more difficulties. Psychological projection occurs when we project an unconscious thought, feeling or experience of our own onto others (*who we've associated with our disowned part*).

For example, you may perceive everyone around you as lazy and selfish and that is the reason you are stuck and never get ahead in life—because they are all too self-absorbed to help you. In reality, if you took a good hard look at yourself, you would likely discover that it is you who tends to be self-centred, self-absorbed, egocentric and inactive.

Growing up, you may have had a parent tell you, *"Stop it! Stop being so naughty! It's embarrassing"* every time you had a little hissy fit because you didn't get your way. And each time you had these meltdowns, your parent repeated their words like a mantra, *"Stop it! Stop being so naughty! It's embarrassing."* As a young child, you put two and two together and began believing that being angry is really bad, wrong and even harmful. But in the moment, you simply felt unheard and unsure as to why that if the parent loves you, could you not have something that makes you happy?

You would then go out of your way to do whatever you could not to get angry. You felt as though being angry was the unsightly thing you could be. With time, you would disassociate from this emotion altogether but—and a big but at that—it doesn't disappear. Conversely, repressing your anger would create the shadow of that very thing.

Let's come back to the present. You are now an adult, and you have grown up believing that one must *'have it all together'* sort of speaking—only to realise you are now experiencing a serious dilemma at work because your colleagues are pushing your buttons and you feel like your head is about to explode.

This is a perfect example of your repressed shadow. When one is experiencing a shadow hissy fit, it is like an explosion of passive-aggressive tones that create an abundance of work issues.

From breakdown to breakthrough...

Because we cannot see our shadow, we might liken it to *'the unconscious mind'*. It is not apparent or evident, and we are largely unaware of its existence. And yet, it is our unconscious mind that controls 95% of our lives.

Likewise, our conscious mind is akin to the light because we can see it clearly and are aware of it. Think of your unconscious mind as the writer, the screenwriter and the author and your conscious mind as the editor, proofreader and evaluator.

You must see the program to reprogram it. But how do we become aware of our programming? When you pay attention, you will realise that the world you see first reveals your unconscious personality. Your triggers, responses and reactions will give you a hint as to your unconscious programs.

Your unconscious mind is just a program and was designed to give you trials. The glory, grandeur and kingdom of the next life will be determined by the way you handle your trials in this life.

All past events, struggles and trials are stored in our bodies as living chemical memories. Although the incident is long over, the chemicals remain. So, each event is alive, awake, and ready to manifest with every reaction to anything and everything that triggers these stored events. You in fact bring the past to your present and experience it as if it is standing right in front of you but maybe with a little bit more fire.

Your unconscious mind can access all memories in the physical body as if they were its own. It's the body-mind connection.

However, there is space between the trigger and response. A tiny window of opportunity to either repeat your previous reactions or refresh them entirely. We have a choice. We have the power to pause, ponder and stay in the space between trigger and response. We can consciously choose to change the meaning and interpretation of the event.

Uncover every part of you that has been disowned...

Our subconscious mind is filled with everything we reject about ourselves—the unacceptable, undesirable, unsatisfactory aspects. Every unwanted bit that you can imagine ends up stashed away in the unconscious mind.

Let me mention it here since it is of great importance for you to understand the difference. Your conscious mind is your awareness of your thoughts and actions. Your subconscious mind is your emotional reactions because it is linked to the limbic part of your brain and your unconscious mind is where all of your repressed memories and past events reside.

Whenever you say or think anything about yourself that is awful, unacceptable, lousy, poor, or bad, you have every reason to suppress, ignore or deny its very existence. Although your shadow is invisible, undetectable, or unnoticed, it hears, feels, lingers and impacts everything that you do—and I do mean everything!

Here's the pinch. Whenever we refuse, reject, or deny any aspect of ourselves, it doesn't disappear or evaporate into thin air. It may vanish from our conscious awareness, but it remains in our unconscious mind. Another analogy I like to use is that you stash it somewhere in a dark corner of your wardrobe—out of sight, out of mind.

Your shadow has a life of its own—yes, it does! In some cultures, they believe that giving a name to your shadow and calling it out by this name helps you integrate those parts of yourself that you don't want to admit to having.

A quote from the Gospel of Thomas: *"If you bring forth what is within you, what you bring forth will save you. If you do not bring forth what is within you, what you do not bring forth will destroy you."* And this, my friend, should be a big enough motivator to do the deep work because your shadow operates outside of your conscious awareness, in the form of the unconscious and limiting beliefs.

Why is my sh!t coming up?

Have you ever been in a place in life where you were so happy, a place of bliss and a place where everything is going perfect, then, all of a sudden sh!t comes up... feelings and emotions from past events? And you find yourself drowning in a sea of negative thoughts? Well, there is a perfectly good reason for it...

We store emotions and thoughts when we experience pain that we find difficult to deal with. We, therefore, repress them until we are ready to let go of them.

The prime directive of our unconscious mind is to let experiences go, not hang on to them, however, when we cannot deal with them at the time, we repress them. These emotions that we repress will show up as a block in our neural pathways within our nervous system.

When we are in a happy place in life when all is going well for us, we are in a place of flow, a place of non-resistance then this is when our sh!t comes up when we are ready or are in a state to deal with them.

Whilst, at the time, it does not feel pleasing, it is a good thing in that it's stuff that is leaving us... it was repressed emotions or feelings from our past, and now that we're non-resistant, it has naturally surfaced and is on its way out...and once it has left us, the repressed emotions will be gone and can no longer linger within us to manifest into anything further.

Repressed emotions can work anywhere in our physical bodies depending on our focus and how we speak about ourselves. Emotions that are repressed for a long time are the emotions that normally cause physical illness. It is the mind-body connection; health is a state of mind!

Your shadow comes bearing gifts...

Your shadow is filled with potential, gifts, talents, and real gems that haven't been identified, detected or unearthed until now. Your shadow isn't always negative—tremendous things are to be found in your shadow, too.

It can be as simple as noticing the words and phrases you often use. For instance, you may say to someone whom you look up to, *"You are brilliant, successful and very inspirational!"* Now, this sounds harmless, especially if you only do it occasionally. However, if this is a repeating pattern, then it may be something to investigate because when doing shadow work, one must keep an eye out for patterns.

Let's bring it to life with a story to fill in the gaps.

There once was a little girl born in the Alps, south of France, who had a very strong sense of self. She was confident, knew what she liked and disliked and never shunned away from asking for what she wanted. She wasn't afraid to speak her mind and was quite a curious one, always asking lots of questions.

Everyone in the small village said she was a very strong little girl. But she was raised with caretakers that constantly told her, *"Keep it down a little!" "Stop showing off. It's way too much. Behave yourself!"* or *"Don't make a fool of yourself by asking so many questions."* I am sure you are picking up on what I am putting down.

Not knowing any better, this brave little girl represses and rejects those parts of herself that are courageous, bold, daring, vulnerable and confident. Instead, she grows up to be quiet, reserved, gentle, submissive, and well-behaved, but she doesn't understand why her life is so agonising and excruciating. She feels lost, stuck, and puzzled.

The truth of the matter is this: she has suppressed and stifled some important, empowering, and authentic aspects of herself. As a result, she feels divided and detached from her true self.

This, my dearest one, is how the shadow was birthed. Although it's there, lurking within the deep, darkest depths of her unconscious mind, she doesn't quite know what to do about it and how to bring it to the light.

There are many reasons why positive aspects of us are relegated to the shadow. For instance, they may end up there because they are afraid of what people may think, how they will react or what they will say about them. These fears hold you back from being your authentic self.

By the way, that little girl in the south of France was me and I share this story with you because we all have stories and when we do this deep shadow work, I can honestly now say I have no problems with any of those things I once repressed.

We all have two lives...

When we dissociate from parts of the self—a mental process where a person disconnects from their thoughts, feelings, memories, or sense of identity—this dissociation creates an internal split. It's almost like two different people are controlling your life or as if you are living two lives if you will.

This takes me back to a time when I was in my friend's car. This lady is the sweetest soul you could ever meet; she was beyond generous, always there for you, going above and beyond any friendship I've ever experienced.

Anyways, I was sitting on the passenger side and a car had taken a sharp left and cut her off. Well, much to my surprise, I heard her yell from the top of her voice language that I do not dare to repeat. She also made very vulgar hand gestures and at that very moment, I felt like I was sitting in the car with a stranger. She had turned into Linda Blair from *The Exorcist*.

Of course, I freaked out a little and wondered how my friend of 20 years suddenly lost the ability to regulate her emotions. This is a perfect example of the two parts operating in her life. Her shadow part got triggered and took over unconsciously, without her awareness.

Most individuals belittle or underestimate the shadow, thinking that it has no power over them. Quite the contrary, the shadow is dominant, authoritative, and very powerful. Left unchecked, it can turn one's life upside down and inside out, destroying their most cherished relationships.

And guess what? Every time your shadow acts out through you, it grows larger, bigger, and stronger!

Ways to spot your shadow self...

One of my mentors and teachers once explained that separation and division are not natural states; they are unhealed states. That which we push away strives to be integrated again, regardless of how much we wish that it would just go away.

Our goal as human beings is to achieve the healing, integration, wholeness, and reunion of these fragmented parts because your unconscious mind will continually work to bring your attention to integrating those parts.

It does take a lot of courage and accountability to spot your shadow, especially when you have invested most of your life pushing it down, repressing it or restricting its very presence. That is why the late Carl Jung said, *"Shadow work is the path of the heart warrior."*

Your shadow will lurk in your unconscious mind until you transmute it into the light. So, you may as well get cosy with it, get to know it, dance with it and befriend it, so you can collaborate and work together, rather than against one another.

There are many ways to spot your shadow. In this book, I am going to go through the main approaches that I teach in my workshops and the methodologies I have used in my research. I am going to take you through the four primary approaches I use.

Finding patterns is the key to wisdom…

If you take a moment to look at your repeating patterns, they are very evident. It may be in a different timeline, with a different person, at a different place, but the same sh!t keeps cropping up. How often have you found yourself in such a predicament?

The power of finding your repeating patterns in your life is so ever empowering because once you see it—it is ever so hard not to see it again. Let me bring this to life with an example.

When I dared to do the deep work and look back upon the timeline of my life, it was very clear to me that I displayed a particular pattern around personal love relationships. Yep! And the thing that dawned on me was that the common denominator was me.

They were different relationships, at different stages of my life, but the ever-so-prevalent factor was moi! We will go through an activity in the next chapter that will help you uncover your repeating patterns.

These patterns in our lives are expressions of our shadow because our shadow mirrors itself in our realities, desperate to be seen and integrated. Yes, it wants to be seen, heard, valued, and accepted. And if you keep ignoring these patterns, guess what? These shadow aspects of oneself will keep showing up until you acknowledge them, value them, and decide to break the cycle.

Be grateful for your triggers...

Another way to spot your shadow is to notice what rocks your boat—your triggers. And boy, if they are not acknowledged, they can surely send you off on a destructive path.

A trigger is an indication and repression of past trauma.

Now, the trauma is dependent on the eye of the beholder, meaning what one person may deem as a major event, another individual may consider such an event as minor. It is dependent on your perception and interpretation. In a nutshell, trauma is your response to an experience.

For example, if you were a single parent and you had to leave your child with someone, maybe even a stranger, that could be traumatic for you and your child. If your boss yelled at you and you have never had anyone raise their tone of voice in your presence, it could become a traumatic experience.

On the other hand, if you had a verbally abusive parent, every time someone raised their tone at you, it might take you back to a troublesome childhood. Whatever personal situations you encountered in your past stimulate your senses, and your body convinces your mind that you are in danger.

Triggers are very powerful messages that enable you to become conscious that something needs to be brought to light because it is buried deep within you and hidden in your shadow. So, pay attention to your triggers and try to catch them before you act them out.

These powerful emotional reactions are an invitation to delve deeper into our unconscious minds. The best way to make the unconscious conscious is to name your triggers, to work with them, because if you can *'label'* your triggers, you can manage them. You can change the effect they have on you. Most importantly, being mindful allows you to take a step back from your emotional reaction and observe it, instead of living it.

We may become triggered for many reasons. Some common aspects involved in being triggered include (*but are not limited to*):

- Acceptance
- Respect
- Being liked
- Being understood
- Freedom
- Being valued
- Having control
- Safety
- Consistency
- New challenges

Thankfully, we can use different mindfulness strategies to refocus our emotional state when we find ourselves getting triggered. For instance, we can:

- Name our triggers or mood states. We can also say to ourselves, *"Right now, I am feeling X."* This reminds us that, although we are currently experiencing this intense thought or emotion, it won't last forever.
- Focus on our breathing to relax and calm the fight-or-flight response.
- Shift our attention to a specific thought or keyword.
- Ground ourselves by focusing on things we can see, hear, etc. in your immediate environment.

Depending on the individual, using analysis and critical thinking can also help a trigger pass. Analysing ourselves as though we were a character in our favourite movie or TV show can assist us by minimising the degree of overwhelming feelings, allowing us to review ourselves with a clearer mind.

Now, this isn't to dismiss our response to a trigger but to instead re-centre our perspective with an outside point of view. This makes it easier to cope with in the moment—we feel less hurt for a character than we do ourselves. Similar to focusing on our senses, analysis works as a distraction and provides the overworking mind with something else to do while still acknowledging the issue.

With patience and practice, we can learn to calm our emotional reactions and become more mindful. Once we're feeling more centred, we can ask ourselves what messages we might learn from our triggers.

Judgement prevents us from seeing the good...

Judgement is a big one. It is something that many of us are unaware of because it has become a habit—one that can destroy some of our deepest relationships. Judgements blind us from seeing what is truly in front of us. They prevent us from seeing the good in others and the light that resides within them.

Being judgmental comes from an imbalanced and reactive mind that is seeking to protect itself from being hurt by others. Judgement is a comparison of ourselves to others. Sometimes, judging others helps us to feel as though we are safe, and the spotlight is cast onto them instead. Our fears cloud our opinions of others, and this comes out as harsh criticism.

Don't be hard on yourself after reading the previous paragraph. Casting judgement is natural—we all do it—and there are ways to change this habit and show others (*and ourselves*) compassion instead. The trick is this: become conscious of your judgments. What specifically are you judging? What is the label or lens that you have towards this individual, place, or event? How much time do I spend judging this particular situation?

The lens you choose will transform the way you look at things. For example, if you look at someone and tell yourself this individual is a *'coward'*. Then my question to you is, *"What is that an example or a representation of?"* You may think that *'coward'* refers to those who are too afraid to stand in their truth or their light or someone without courage.

Judgement is the absence of love...

One of my repeated judgements was hearing myself say, *"Wow, he or she has a big ego"* or *"Talk about an egoistic individual."* Then my question to myself was, *"What is that an example or representation of?"* Ego for me is an example of someone being confident, with self-worth, self-respect, and self-esteem. It's all about them!

So, the first step is to be clear on the *meaning* of the label that you are pointing out or judging and in what area of your life it occurs. Whatever you judge or point your finger at is your shadow showing you where you can gain greater awareness. In the shadow, we find our little gifts.

Let's go back to my coward story. My shadow was letting me know that I had to be more egotistic in all areas of my life. Not selfish or arrogant but more self-full, starting to think about myself a little more. Starting to believe in myself, back myself and know that I was worthy of such positive attention. Well, that was a big etheric slap! It woke me up as to why I was continuously throwing that judgement around.

The more time we invest into understanding what, who and why we judge, the more likely we will experience insightful breakthroughs. You may become aware of what you have been carrying around for such a long time. The shadow is our greatest teacher. If we listen carefully, we can use our triggers for greater self-awareness and self-compassion.

One of the biggest mistakes you can make when partaking in shadow work is to cast judgement on what you have identified. If you let the grim inner critic emerge and judge the shadow, you are rejecting it all over again and consequently, making it bigger and stronger.

Perception equals projection...

The last and probably the hardest thing to accept and admit is our projections. We are always—and I do mean *always*—projecting our sh!t, issues, and frustration onto others. It is the stuff that we dislike, disown, and disapprove of in ourselves.

Rather than own it and work with it, it is so much easier to point the finger and blame everything external to ourselves. What we don't realise is this: when we are pointing a finger at another, we have three pointing right back at us. Now, what is that telling you?

We often project our shadows (*which come in the form of our repressed anger, guilt, shame, and other things we don't like about ourselves*) onto others. We criticise, chastise, and lash out at people for their behaviours that we don't like in ourselves.

Change your perception of things and you will change your reality. The difference in how each person perceives a situation is a projection of what is going on inside them. You will only perceive the things that you have within *you*. You can't see things if they don't exist or reside within your mind.

Perceptions don't always have to be negative, such as when you are around people or situations that motivate you or lift your spirits. In these scenarios, you are recognising those qualities within yourself. But you must get curious when you are triggered or react to certain things in your environment. Your triggers are a source of wisdom for you.

So, the next time you find yourself around a person that annoys or delights you or you find yourself in a situation where you are going to make a judgement about something, ask yourself, *"How is this a reflection of myself?"* Pay attention to how you project yourself into the outside world because the Universe works to make us whole again. People, places, and things become a mirror and reflect who we truly are.

Don't shame or blame your shadow...

It's so easy, when things go wrong, to blame other people. Whether it's something as simple as being late or a big stuff up, we're all guilty of wanting to find a scapegoat. Part of the reason we do this is because it's easier to be mad at someone else than it is to be mad at ourselves.

But you know what? When you blame someone else, you give up your power. *You* become the victim. Say what? Yes. It's true. Rather than admit they have done something wrong, people go to amazing lengths to paint themselves as poor, innocent bystander who never has to take responsibility.

Every single human being you meet is fighting a battle that you know nothing about—stewing over an argument with their spouse, on day three of a diet and battling with the new regime, worrying about a health problem or the health of a loved one, nervous about a child sitting exams today. We're all intrinsically linked, and we all have a story that's our own, which is also interwoven with the people we love and care for.

You can see why so many individuals resist shadow work. There is nowhere to hide, there is no blaming, shaming, or playing the victim. You must own your sh!t 100%. And when you do, it is the most emancipating, freeing, life-changing and profound experience.

Your shadow is part of who you are. So, rather than alienate, irritate, or antagonise it, be open to the messages from your shadow, accept it with open arms and look at it from a place of love.

Resistance is the first step to change...

Although it can take time, it is wise to make peace with your shadow. If you feel a little resistance, in case you fear what you may find, then this is a sure sign that you must do the deep work and befriend your shadow.

When you are in a place of resistance, you are resisting an aspect of yourself. But the more you resist the self, the greater it becomes. The more energy you focus on pushing it away, the larger it becomes. Resistance means the refusal to accept or comply with something; it is hiding or denying an aspect of the self.

We all have a shadow side. We are yin and we are yang; we are descending and we are ascending; we are light and we are dark; we are Anima and we are Animus. There is a duality that resides within us, which makes us who we are as a whole.

Power of self comes when you truly embrace the resistance, embrace your shadow side, and integrate it into the light. It is the only way to achieve balance and freedom. Shadow work is making the unconscious conscious and the unacceptable acceptable. The whole purpose of this book and shadow work is to integrate and bring your shadow into the light to shine.

In the remaining chapters, we will go through step-by-step how to integrate and shine a light on the beautiful shadow aspect of yourself. This part of you that is fractured, injured, broken, or crippled in some way is seeking to become unified, united, and whole.

Chapter 2
Harness the Power of Patterns…

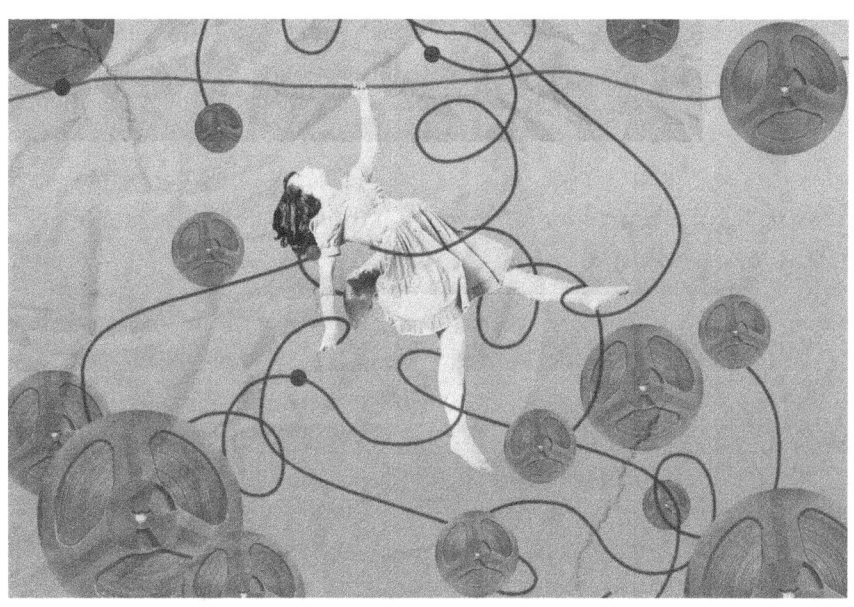

"There is no greater agony than bearing an untold story inside you" – **Maya Angelou**

Life is a book; full of blank pages that we are destined to fill with our life events. You see, we all have stories, some more or less than others. Regardless of the value, we apply to these stories, it's more important what we decide to do with them. These stories are either never-ending journeys, suppressed memories, hidden talents or repeating patterns that we can no longer dismiss.

Stories regarding repeating patterns hold the answer to things about yourself that you have yet to unfold. If only we had the insight to notice them, instead of allowing our minds to hit replay. As you read the previous two sentences, what immediately comes to mind? Whatever the answer may be, hold onto that as you flow through this chapter.

Interestingly, humanity has used stories from the beginning of time to connect communities and create movements, from cave drawings to campfire tales. It makes you wonder what many of the unwritten stories could have been about. Who was involved? And what message would the story send?

Even in the digital age, stories continue to be committed to memory and passed on from generation to generation through a combination of illustrative, oral, and written formats.

Fairy tales, short stories, and mythology link people to history. They have taught us specific lessons such as *'slow and steady wins the race'*, which most of us know from *'The Hare and the Tortoise'*. Such stories are utilised in our everyday experience, often in the form of a moral handbook.

Why stories affect us at an incredibly deep intellectual and emotional level is something that neuroscience is just beginning to understand. Scientists have discovered that fictional stories affect the same region of the brain that reacts when we are engaged in a real-life event.

Stories create a bonding empathy that causes us to strongly identify with the characters as if we were living the character's experiences ourselves. On an unconscious level–stories impact us to the point where our brain is confused as to what is real and what is not real.

We know that our brain exhibits the following:

- It cannot easily remember a large amount of data with no context. For instance, it is much easier to remember a story about your friend's bad experience at the grocery store, than it is to recall ten random facts.
- Our brain can only hold about seven pieces of information for less than 30 seconds at a time.
- Short attention span–can only focus for 10 minutes at a time before it tunes out.
- Love for repetition–requires to be told the same message repeatedly so that it remembers, and then can analyse the information to store it in memory.

Remember to think of your unconscious mind as the writer, the screenwriter and the author and your conscious mind as the editor, proofreader, and evaluator of your stories.

When we deny our stories, they define us...

There is something in us, as storytellers and as listeners to stories, that demands the redemptive act. By that I mean everyone at some point desires that whatever is lost, must be given a shot at restoration. Movie endings are a prime example because they require the protagonist's problem to be resolved in order to have an ending. The need to fix and resolve things is ingrained in human nature. But what if I told you that *'brokenness'* is an overused concept that does not apply to us as individuals? What if I told you there was nothing to fix? Then what?

We have all experienced what it's like to feel stuck. Sometimes getting unstuck is a simple matter of shifting the stories that we are telling ourselves. Highlight this—the only reason we feel stuck is that we are disconnected from our own authentic needs, feelings, and callings. Yep, you heard that right. Feeling stuck is a result of misalignment with what we want in life and our current unwillingness to go after it.

Yet our narratives serve a purpose, and it is up to us to unravel why we keep repeating these stories. It is up to us to seek why we continuously trip over and relive them over and over again. We must acknowledge the need to break the pattern.

We have to put our detective hats on and decode their meaning to determine why they appear from the unconscious mind. Why do they want to be validated, felt, or seen? And yet... Why do these self-defeating stories steal our happiness by preventing us from exploring new possibilities such as trying that mysterious place to eat on the corner, asking our friend on a date or simply having more spontaneous adventures? Why do we as humans take everything so seriously?

Creativeness is finding patterns...

Finding repeating patterns isn't as hard as you think. The very core of these patterns will reveal your hidden stories that want to be seen, heard, and felt. Remember the stories I told you to hold onto earlier in this chapter? Have those with you and try your best to include them now as I ask you to hover over your timeline. It is time to discover as many patterns as possible as we look back at our past and life as a person, to know where it may be heading into the future.

Your timeline is an internal guiding system; your treasure map if you will. Only once you know the direction you should take, then you can start to virtually hover over your timeline. Now, the best way to do this is not through your rational mind but your creative mind, otherwise known as the right side of your brain. This is where all your intuition, hunches and magical ideas rise to the surface.

Let's give it a go, shall we? Get comfortable in a chair, close your eyes, and choose which direction your past timeline is in. Now imagine jumping on an old, rickety sailing boat surrounded by rough, midnight blue seas. Then imagine this scene appearing before your third eye, otherwise referred to as your state of higher spiritual awakening and intuition. Once you have completed this vision, then allow yourself to sail this boat into the clouds above the land and ocean, maintaining a bird's eye view of your timeline. Keep in mind your mission is to find the patterns, that's it.

Values are like lighthouses...

Renowned sociologist, Dr Morris Massey, described three major periods during our lives where values are developed. Following the development of our values, our stories then come to life for the first time. Whilst our values change and develop over time as we age and mature, this very collapse of our values system gives our stories a different life and form.

Massey explains it this way, *"What you are is where you were when... again!"* This relates to the first part of our development, known as the imprinting phase, from the time we are born right up to the age of 7. It is inclusive of all your experiences up to that age, such as your relationship with parents or guardians, siblings, and friends. All the things you watched on television, the things you heard, and read or any encounters you experienced at that time were imprinted on you.

The best analogy I have for this is to imagine you are a computer. All the software (*experiences*) that you downloaded onto your hard drive, have formed your stories, values, and beliefs.

The next chapter of your life from 7 to 14 is the modelling phase. This chapter addresses who you look up to, who inspired you and who you aspired to be. In this phase, we seek external of ourselves to find our identity and quite often this comes in the form of copying those that we admire. We may end up looking like them, speaking like them and modelling their behaviours and mannerisms.

Value and accept who you are...

Massey explains that 90% of our values are set by the time we reach 10 years old. If you can go back in time to that place, try to see if what you are connecting with and what you remember is evident in your life today. You can see how knowing and associating with those very important memories helps bring your patterns into awareness.

The third and final chapter that Massey speaks about is the socialisation phase, occurring between the ages of 14 to 21. I like to call this one the rebellious phase. We have all experienced it and for those that have children, when they hit this chapter of their life the best thing you can do is to be a friend rather than a parent.

Socialisation is when one rebels against their parents and values. They feel as though they are burdened by the same expectations that have always been imposed, as they have collected new ways of perceiving the world. In order to grasp these new ideas, one rushes into rejecting their home and chooses to leave the nest to determine the place of their new identity in society.

This is where they become part of an external group. Whether it is through social media, college or hobbies, the end goal is to find belonging. At this phase of one's life, one can get caught up in religion, a genre of music, the news around the world and other groups from the collective that may have been foreign before.

Your story timeline memories...

Massey explains that by the age of 20 your values are 100% locked in for life. The only thing that can change these set values is a significant emotional event, either at a personal or global level. Think about it this way. When you were a teenager what did you value the most? Compare this to now as an adult. Are these values still important to you? As you can see things change and if we go back to our timeline, we will see the repeating patterns in the things that are important to us.

During your journey back in time, what may become prevalent are significant events from your life that impacted you in some way and helped shape the person you are today. There may be individuals such as teachers, mentors, coaches, bosses, partners, friends, family and even enemies that have either influenced or left an impression as though they are still beside you.

Let's call this impression an invisible guide. I know what you are thinking, why would I want to carry an enemy around with me as an invisible friend? We will unpack that a little bit more in another chapter where we take a good look at your inner critic because we all have one that shows up for us. Then there are the major events that you can pull out some of the most spectacular stories from your timeline, such as a story of coming of age, a crisis story, battles in relationships, happy or challenging childhood—but my question to you is what did you learn from each event? Do you even see these events as learning opportunities? Or do you view them as mere blessings or pointless tragedies?

Deconstruct and rebuild your story...

It's time to get curious about the very construction of your story. Too often we immerse ourselves in the events of everyone else's story that we lose interest in our own. Our story then becomes disengaging because we are familiar with it but in reality, we are just stuck. And the only way to get unstuck and narrate a story we are proud of is to find the patterns.

These patterns are not just physical or ecological patterns, they can be thinking patterns, they can be self-talk patterns and they can be patterns of self-sabotage and the list goes on...

All these experiences have influenced your mindset, your belief system, your set of assumptions and most importantly your habits! Habits of the mind are formed by previous experiences. They are patterns of thinking that determine how we make sense of the world. Our mindset has an impact on how we behave, and what actions we take and in turn, this has an impact on how we relate to others.

We can be so fixated with other individuals, comparing ourselves to others but how often do we stop to think and acknowledge that everyone has their own story and challenges? What they have achieved is only one piece of their life. You must reinforce to yourself that you are not in competition with everyone else around you.

Capture the spirit of the times...

Did you know that your environment shapes who you are? Yep! Be careful, for the environment you choose will shape you. Our friend Winston Churchill declares that *"we shape our buildings; thereafter they shape us."* It's true. Here's why.

We know from research that our environment shapes us from the time we are born. Consequently, in many ways, it shapes our personality. However, our personality is not our identity. Our personality is a combination of characteristics, patterns, or qualities that we have learned and obtained from our social environment.

Mindfulness is awareness of your surroundings and how they influence you. The more mindful you become, the more you realise you don't have to allow the environment you are in to control your mood or how you feel. When you know that who you are is totally influenced by your situation, you take a lot more ownership of that situation and how it determines your thoughts and behaviours.

Look around you, read your surroundings, symbolically and ask yourself, *"How was your story shaped?" "What was your influence?" "What environment influenced your emotions the most?"* Many of us become immersed in external events or physical surroundings and lose touch with our own nature, place, and their own existence in the world. We are very much conditioned by our environment. Dr Bruce Lipton talks about this in relation to his 3-petri dish experiment, where he places the exact same cell in each petri dish. The only thing that changed was the environment. And guess what? The cells changed and became dependent on their environment.

Be greater than your environment...

Don't let the environment dictate what you do, who you are, or who you will become. Personally, what I have learned over the years is this: you can invest all the time, energy, and care in the world toward an individual. However, if they are not in the right environment, meaning one that is supportive, nurturing and aligned with them and their values, well... it will become increasingly more difficult to speed up their progress.

Environment plays a huge part in how we show up and what we become. Albert Einstein tells us that *"the environment is everything that isn't me."* With this approach in mind, why are we so conditioned by our environment? It is too easy to let our environment promote or impair us.

Environment plays a huge part in how we show up and what we become. For example, let's say you are working in an environment where there has been constant change. You, on the other hand, are the type of person who values order, consistency, and stability. As a result, you will automatically behave in a way that is conforming to the environment because you are driven by *'fear'*. The same goes for dynamic individuals stuck in a static environment.

We all know from our primitive brains that all human beings have a strong need for *'safety'* and *'security'*. Also, we know that we tend to seek some sort of physical comfort in any environment. In addition to that, we search for an environment that is psychologically comfortable, an environment that feels familiar... one that offers the right amount of stimulus.

Therefore, the environment can facilitate or discourage interactions among individuals, also affecting how they show up. Any given environment has the power to influence certain behaviours and, consequently, outcomes. Your aim is to have an environment that is at a steady pace, an environment that can influence people's behaviours in a positive way.

Life is your biggest treasure...

So, welcome to the movie of your life!

Treasure, love, reward, approval, honour, freedom, and survival are just a few of the many experiences one can endure in the hero's journey. But ... in finding our little treasure most times there is an initiation process for us to get those golden moments.

These initiations come in all shapes and forms. If we look at our own initiations—for example, when I consider my own—some of my deep unspeakable sufferings and battles with inner and outer demons, were my transformation. Quite simply, I wouldn't be who I am today without the experience. That in itself is an initiation. In the hero's journey, there is a very colourful metaphor that symbolises a significant purpose. The hero rescuing the long-haired princess from her mother in the tall, forest tower; for you, this could be confronting someone who is a bully or giving birth to a child is a profound initiation in itself.

Initiations are about pushing through and confronting whatever you are afraid of. It's about getting uncomfortable, and only then can we go through a self-discovery of what we are capable of. We must not fear, fear itself, but look at fear as a passage or a bridge to get to the other side.

The hero's journey to empowerment...

Author and mythologist Joseph Campbell wrote a seminal work, *'The Hero with a Thousand Faces'* (1949) which became *'Hero's Journey, a Monomyth'* ... and rather than be the victim of your story, we are going to flip it and see how you are the hero of your story. Remember it is the meaning we give our story to whether our story is going to be grandiose, extravagant, or monumental.

The ordinary world is where the hero's journey begins. In stories and films, the ordinary world is the environment in which the hero is introduced to the audience. We learn about their background and their everyday world—where they live, the people in their lives and the routines that keep life comfortable. In *'real life'* the ordinary world is where many people exist. It is the place where life is often quite comfortable but not necessarily satisfying, a place neither challenging nor exciting, a place where life has seemed to reach a kind of plateau.

The ordinary world is a useful transitory place to rest and recover, however, remaining there permanently results in a lack of growth and new experiences. This is the place where people become complacent, apathetic, stifled, and stagnant—and often don't even realise they exist in the ordinary world until they are faced with the opportunity to leave it. And leaving it can be improbably terrifying.

Questions to help frame this step:

- You feel it, don't you? That there should be something more. But what is it?
- You have a destiny, a calling... Can you hear it? What does it say?
- Where are you right now in your life? Is it where you want to be? Where do you visualise yourself?
- Do you get the sense that something's just not quite right, that something needs to be changed?
- Maybe it's not about the external environment; do you feel that it's you who needs changing?
- If you were to disappear tomorrow and despite that being tragic, would you be satisfied with everything you have become in life?

Listen to the voice that separates you from your ordinary world, because it is asking you to take a step further on your hero's journey. When you can describe in your own words what your ordinary world looks like and why you do what you do, it will be a paradigm shift.

The call to adventure awaits...

"The BIG question is whether you are going to be able to say a hearty yes to your adventure" –
Joseph Campbell.

Life sometimes has a funny way of calling us towards our truth. Sometimes it comes quietly knocking ... perhaps even several times. More often than not, it arrives with a big bang! In this next phase of the hero's journey, the call to adventure is an event that interrupts the comfort of the ordinary world, and the hero (*you*) is forced to meet with change.

The call to adventure in a person's life is when they are first given notice that everything is going to change, whether they know it or not. It may be an external or internal event such as a yearning, a feeling of dissatisfaction, frustration, curiosity, ambition, or intuition about something you must pursue.

Think of yourself as Indiana Jones ... and get ready for adventure! Transformation takes time. And step-by-step it tests our resilience, over and over and over again! But ... When we hang in there and fight for what we desire, the result is incredibly rewarding and is awarded much sooner than you may think.

When the world as we know it is no longer fulfilling or endurable, when there is a crisis, or when a door closes, we are '*called forth*' to step into a higher purpose. The call brings up the curtain, always on the mystery of transfiguration. The familiar life horizon has been outgrown; the old concepts, ideals, and emotional patterns no longer fit; the time for passing the threshold is at hand.

When there is doubt, fear, lack of self-belief, lack of self-worth, and lack of self-trust—it simply means that you don't back yourself. You physically have turned your back away from you. Why not try to turn to yourself, face yourself, lean into yourself ... with compassion, understanding, forgiveness and connection to the self and see where it takes you.

A true initiation never ends...

So, if the first phase of your adventure is where there is a departure from your ordinary world, then the call to do something—could be your first child, your first business, or your first home, where you have limited awareness of your role in this new world. It could also be an end of a relationship, an end of a career, or a transition in life such as retirement. This is your destiny calling when you have made your decision, either way, you are now being called forward to take the adventure, it is literally knocking at your door—this is the call to the unknown.

This part of your adventure might be a premonition where there is an increase in awareness of the need to change. Let's say you embark on a new business venture, you may bump into the right person who may guide you along your path to help you clarify your treasure, and what you are searching for ... helping you define your goals and bringing them to life.

If you feel called to something greater than what your current job or life offers—this means you are being called forward to embark on your hero's journey of transformation. Your own metamorphosis.

Stepping into the unknown to find your calling or to answer a call may involve:

- Facing the fear of the unknown, uncertainty or obstacles
- Finding your true self and your transforming idea
- Integrating your vision into your life and work

Joseph Campbell was an inquisitive and curious mythologist. Instead of focusing on the differences between cultural myths, he explored and searched for the similarities, where his findings resulted in what's called the monomyth, which is a universal story structure – a story template that takes a character through a sequence of stages. Like a movie.

Questions to help frame this step:

- Wherever you are in your journey, what is it that's calling you to step out into a new world right now?
- Is it something you're no longer willing to accept?
- Is it something that no longer serves you, but you don't know how to get out of the rut?
- Is it a new goal you need to set for yourself?
- What's the treasure you're after?
- What in your life is calling you to a new adventure?
- Is it because of something someone has said?

The call to adventure is what happens to prompt the hero to take a step into the adventure. For me, it was the increased awareness that something needed to be changed. Something shakes up the situation, either from external pressures or from something rising up deep from within, so the hero must face the beginnings of change.

Sometimes during the call to adventure, a messenger arrives, a portent call, and there is reluctance or suspicion but a knowing, increased awareness of the need for change.

The refusal of the call...

Often when the call is given, the future hero refuses to heed it. This may be from a sense of duty, obligation or fear, disbelief, insecurity, a sense of inadequacy or any of a range of reasons that work to hold the person in his or her current circumstances.

It is this phase of your adventure where you may feel the experience of resistance, you may question yourself, doubt what you are doing, feeling in fear of where you are going. This is where the hero refuses the call, it is a natural part of our cycle in everything that we do. And this is when one may fall victim to their own mind ... Some people create their own storms and then get angry when it rains. When you are in this phase of your journey, you seek a way out because you are experiencing pain in your world.

But ... this is when you must push forward!

If you question and challenge the refusal of the call, why does the hero (*you*) refuse to go? Is this fear or resistance? It will become very apparent when you resist or refuse the call because your mind will go out of its way to find a reason or a better way of doing the very thing you must do. For example, the hero refuses the call by changing direction, going the easy route. In our world it may be as simple as people wanting to leave the system but are afraid to do so, whether they are bored, compromising their values, working hard, or trying to find a way to escape.

Questions to help frame this step:

- Where are you experiencing pain in your world?
- Where are you feeling stuck in your world?
- What obstacles are available for you to push you forward?
- Can you see or feel your adventure?
- Are you refusing the call?
- If so, what motivates the refusal?

Obligation and duty, fear, a sense of inadequacy to take on the quest, and dread or dislike of the task to be taken on are all reasons the hero may refuse the call. The hero feels the fear of the unknown and tries to turn away from the adventure, however briefly. Alternatively, another character may express the uncertainty and danger ahead.

Courage is resistance to fear...

And... then my friend you are rewarded with the next part of your adventure, overcoming your fear. This is where you choose your path, stay on your path and once you are sure with every ounce of your being, you will magically create miracles to help you along your merry way. It could be a mentor to guide you in the right direction. It could be finding an investor for your business; it could be finding the person who can help you make appropriate connections for your new journey. It could be anything really that you need right now!

When you do this, as the hero (*not the victim*) of your own life, you're propelled forward into the adventure. Once the hero has committed to the quest, consciously or unconsciously, their guide and magical helper appears or becomes known.

Meeting with the mentor can be as simple as the hero gaining supernatural aid, assistance, or a miracle. The hero is encouraged by a wise, older person or artefact which will help them along their way, which helps the hero gain wisdom.

Questions to help frame this step:

- What special friends or helpers do you have as the hero of your story?
- Who would be that one individual to help you prepare to leave on your journey?
- Is it a one-time assistance, or will the helper/s appear throughout your journey?
- Who would make a good accountability partner to support you on your journey?
- Why are they a suitable partner?
- Who would you choose to be the wise mentors in your hero's journey, and what would they tell you?

The mentor comes across a seasoned traveller of the world who gives the hero training, equipment, or advice that will help on the journey. And thus, the hero reaches within for a source of courage, endurance, and wisdom.

As you think about the treasure you're after in this journey, who are the wise mentors you could use? In this day and age, we're surrounded by an abundance of mentors, either people you can meet in person, talk over the phone, through the internet, or books, videos and audio programs from experts you haven't even met, from across the globe, who can give you instant advice.

As you go across your day, keep your eyes and ears open. Notice what mentors *'magically'* pop out to give you advice that you can use. Is it going to be someone you meet? It could be a song you overhear, a quote you stumble across or a niche online course you never knew existed.

It takes a big commitment to change...

German writer, Johann Wolfgang von Goethe, reminds us that *"the moment one definitely commits oneself, and then providence moves too."*

All sorts of things occur to help—and these are things that would never otherwise have occurred. A whole stream of events arises from the decision, raising all manner of unforeseen incidents, meetings, and material assistance that no person could have dreamed would have come their way. Many self-help gurus, spiritual writers and philosophers talk about this—it's about creating momentum. Once you back yourself, the Universe starts to back you too.

This is the next part of your adventure when you are committed to the change. It is where the hero must pass a trial, crossing the limits of the known into the unknown. We are hardwired to resist change. Our brain is on the watch out to keep us safe, constantly looking for anything that may endanger us. As a result, it seeks negativity. Keeping this in mind when committing to change is of great importance.

Questions to help frame this step:

- Are there people you have to meet, places you have to go, and things you have to do that are outside of your comfort zone?
- Are there fears and doubts that you have to overcome inside of yourself?
- What world is being left? What world is being entered?
- What or who is guarding the threshold?

- What obstacles must the hero overcome to truly begin the journey? Limits of home or society, limits of personality, limits of perception, physical limits?
- What is the threshold and how does the individual cross the threshold?

Commitment is an act, not a word. Commitment is that turning point in your life when you accept the moment and transmute it into an opportunity to transform your destiny. One of my favourite teachers would always say to stay committed to your decisions but always stay flexible in your approach. This takes a lot of adaptivity, agility and dexterity.

All of life is an experiment...

Being the creator of your life, growing and taking risks in life ... making mistakes, learning from them, and having fun—is all about experimenting with your life. This is the next stage of your adventure, this is where you experiment with your new conditions, and this is where the hero undergoes a series of trials.

We need to keep in mind that life in itself is a pattern and sometimes when we are in the thick of life, we are not aware of our patterns. In this phase of your adventure, it's important to pay attention to these patterns, because most of the time these patterns are unconscious. If we don't address them, we can be condemned to repeat them.

Once the hero has begun their journey, they will soon encounter various tests. Various characters will appear during the tests and will either test or assist you. Often the hero will meet a mentor who will offer assistance in clarifying the hero's value system—what it is they stand for and the type of person they want to be. Often the mentor becomes one of the most powerful allies on the journey, particularly when the hero may appear to have lost their way.

Questions to help frame this step:

- What kind of trials and ordeals make sense to you and what would be truly challenging?
- What do you fear and how will this fear appear or be represented to you?
- What do you as the hero consider to be obstacles to progress or growth?
- Do you have some personality or character traits that will be mirrored back to you in a challenging way?
- What strategies, skills, insights, or talents can you use to resolve these trials?
- What assistance do you have to deal with these trials?

As the hero travels and experiments with new conditions, they undergo a series of tests and trials.

There are two ways to understand the concept of test, enemies, and allies. The first is a literal understanding, that there are characters or people who will help us along the way and there will be those who will only make things harder for us. However, a more powerful way to understand this concept is by seeing it as a metaphor for accepting responsibility for our own actions.

If it doesn't challenge you, it won't change you...

The next part of your adventure is where the hero enters the inmost cave that holds all your memories and habits. This is where the hero encounters an affirming love who has knowledge and wisdom that will help the hero complete the transition.

If you thought the previous parts of your journey were testing, well, they were only preparing you for this, because this is where the deep work begins. This is the time to unpack your limiting beliefs, what you are self-sabotaging and any behaviours that are not conducive to who you want to be, do or have.

Self-sabotage. If you're into self-help and spirituality, this is a term that comes up a lot. But what exactly does it mean? Self-sabotage is when we say we want something and then we go out of our way to make sure it doesn't happen. When your unconscious mind thinks it's not *'worthy'* of success, happiness, or freedom, it will sabotage that very thing you want. Normally this takes place when you have a certain level of finance, love, success, or connection. And it shows up in many ways, it could be as simple as procrastination or we make up excuses as to *'why'* we are avoiding exercise, drinking too much, being unhealthy or obsessive thinking with no action.

Questions to help frame this step:

- What are your dysfunctional behaviours, limiting beliefs or self-sabotage?
- Hero, villain, or victim, who are you rescuing?
- What behaviours, attitudes, relationships, and dependencies must you let go of or sacrifice?
- Is there someone you have been putting off having a courageous conversation with?
- Is there a situation that's been difficult but you're avoiding facing?
- What limiting beliefs are slowing you down?

And ... as if to test your resolve, it's usually at the next part of your journey when you're really faced with temptation. It's generally a path that leads you away from the quest! This was me ten years ago when I embarked on a new adventure to start my own business. Twelve months in, I was offered an amazing role that paid a lot more than what I was currently earning. Of course, that moment makes you question what you're doing .... But is it time to give it all up now? Is that how your movie script plays out?

We gain strength when we resist temptation...

Okay, so yes, it was very tempting, but the very thing that stopped me from taking that job was a book I was reading at the time. And it's true that *'when we are three feet from gold – the temptation is revealed'*.

This is simply another test. But it could be the biggest you've faced so far.

The only thing you know for sure at this point is that you must completely let go. If you're serious about the desire to transform your life that started this whole journey, then you must let go of your old self too. In many ways, it's only through the death of the self that you can experience a rebirth or renewal that is causing you to contemplate the change. Nature does this all the time. You can too.

> *"Conquering temptation represents a new form of moral energy. Every trial endured and weathered is the right spirit that makes a soul nobler and stronger than it was before"* –
> **William Butler Yeats**.

At this point, the most important thing you need to ask yourself, is *"who or what do I need to confront that is holding me back?"* And maybe it's a good time to pause too. Take a rest to digest the insights and allow the integration of change to take place.

Questions to help frame this step:

- What do you fear the most in life?
- Who do you need to confront? What battle do you need to let go of?
- What strengths do you have that you can use for this ordeal as the hero of your journey?
- What are the goals that have been accomplished and which ones are holding you back?
- What breaks, rests, pauses, or moves do you have to take to restore your strengths?
- What do you experience now that is beyond, good and evil, or even life and death?

It is a key moment when the hero finally faces their innermost fear and overcomes it. The hero is often propelled into this battle when they understand that the consequence of ignoring the fear is far greater than failing.

However, beneath all these types of battles, we must face our greatest fear. By doing so, we will learn the greatest lesson about ourselves and that this is the ultimate purpose of the journey. In real life, the hero's journey translates as a powerful lesson—one about self-acceptance and letting go of the ego during battle. The hero usually embraces death to self and experiences a rebirth or renewal of the cause by suffering through the ordeal.

Life's biggest rewards come from the biggest challenges...

In the next phase of your adventure, you are rewarded and liberated from both the inner and outer demons of your old world. Victory often comes with a struggle to stay and not to return to the *'old world'* or *'old ways'* of working or being.

This is where the hero may let go of all conflict and reconcile with the things that they had to endure and overcome. The hero puts away his sword because the final battle was conquered. This phase is crucial for you to celebrate and reward yourself for the changes that you've made, and the victory that you have accomplished.

In this phase of the adventure, the hero leaves the scene of victory and sometimes a new problem arises that is just as bold, where the enemy may rise for one last battle. This is another test to see how many more fights you have in you. You decide whether you are worth the reward.

Decide that you are. Keep going. Keep strong. Keep steady.

Questions to help frame this step:

- What is your ultimate reward that is within your grasp? Is that reward worth it?
- What are you worth?

- When did you last reward yourself for change made, and victory accomplished?
- What areas of your life are you recognised when going above and beyond?
- What areas of your life do you feel valued and appreciated?
- What type of reward and recognition do you value the most?

Victory often comes with a backlash, a counterpoint such as not wishing to return to the normal world. The hero now lives with the knowledge that they have the ability to endure whatever they experience in life. In the end, no matter the battle, the reward is almost always the same where the hero learns to surrender to life and to love, always loving and accepting themselves for who they truly are.

Challenges are what makes life interesting...

Be thankful for every new challenge. Each will give you more strength, wisdom, and character. We don't grow when things are easy, we grow when we face challenges. Being open to new ideas, opportunities, and challenges will keep you thinking, dreaming, and increasing your level of imagination to meet the new challenge head-on with dedication.

This is the next phase of the hero's adventure, where you must finally prepare to cross the threshold of return. The road back. This is where you must go back to the ordinary world, your old world, but with a new lens. And then you realise that you have changed forever. Since you are no longer the person you were once before, returning home forces you to align your ordinary world with your newfound world.

Questions to help frame this step:

- Since you are no longer the person you used to be... what must change *'back home'*?
- Who are you now? What's your life plan look like now?
- What new challenges and re-dedication is the hero experiencing?

- How does the hero attempt to return to their normal life?
- Are you concerned that your message won't be heard?
- Are you worried that your gifts will be unappreciated? Or that your wisdom gained cannot be communicated?

What you allow is what will continue. Boundaries grant you access to get more of what you want and less of what you don't want. A person with healthy boundaries can say *'no'* to others whenever they want to, without feeling guilty. They protect and honour the space that they have created to clarify what behaviours are acceptable and unacceptable from others. And as the hero of your story, one must set strong boundaries so as not to go back to your old ways of being.

The awakening does not come to you. You find it in you...

There is an overwhelming sensation that's occurring deep inside of you. You question everything. You trust only a few people. You no longer believe in everything that was sold to you as a kid. You're looking for facts, proof, and for undeniable consistencies. This is proof that you are transforming, and awakening; don't fight it. Allow this energy to flow.

And then there is the next path to your adventure. The return to the normal world ... Your old world involves an awakening, a rebirth, or a resurrection, where the hero may be pulled out of their adventure by a force external to themselves. Sometimes when we have gone through a shift, we have a different understanding and knowledge about life. When you share these thoughts with old friends, they may try to talk you out of them, or they may try to pull you back into the old ordinary world.

Questions to help frame this step:

- How will you use your learnings for the benefit of others? To whom will you impart your newfound knowledge and experience?

- What are the obstacles or the final test to returning home?
- Will these obstacles further enlighten you about either a person, the quest, or blessings?
- What final battle may you need to face? Is there another step in this journey that you need to take in order to feel as though you are 'home' and able to integrate everything you've learned in your life?
- What would it take to embrace your new self 100%?

At the climax, the hero is severely tested once more on the threshold of the home. They are purified by a last sacrifice, another moment of death and rebirth, but on a higher and more complete level. Through the hero's action, the polarities that were in conflict at the beginning are finally resolved. The return to the normal world involves an awakening, rebirth, resurrection, or emergence. The hero may be pulled out of their adventure by a force external to themselves.

Mastery is a product of consistently going beyond our limits…

This my friend is the final phase of your adventure. Mastery is the path of patience and dedicated effort without attachment to immediate results. Self-mastery is a challenge for every individual … It is the ultimate test of our character. It requires climbing out of the deep valleys of our lives and scaling our own Mount Everest …

> *"In its simplest terms, self-mastery is doing those things we should do and not doing those things we should not do. It requires strength, willpower, and honesty"* –**James Faust**.

The hero is now the master of two worlds, the inner and outer world, with the understanding that everything around you is a reflection of this internal world.

There is now balance and freedom to live one's life, on one's own terms. The hero is no longer afraid of the unknown because the hero understands that the journey itself leads to freedom.

The hero returns home or continues the journey, bearing some element of the treasure that has the power to transform the world as the hero has been transformed. The hero is no longer afraid of the unknown, of the spiritual. Mastery leads to freedom from death, and freedom to live.

Questions to help frame this step:

- Are you really ready to put your feet up?
- What is your next adventure? Where's the next mountain?
- What is the elixir you are bringing back with you from your journey? Who are you going to share it with?
- How are you going to pay forward what you learned? What difference are you going to make in the world?
- What knowledge or wisdom are you bringing back to share?
- Will there be any haters or doubters? If so, how can you remind yourself that you didn't do it for them, you did it because it was your destiny to be the hero of your own life.

.... And it's at that very moment, that you are up for the next challenge, the next adventure!

The hero's journey is about following your heart and listening to those little niggles—or that soft voice of your intuition encouraging you to take the first step.

A little bit like the unfolding of the yellow brick road, with every step forward, the yellow brick road unfolds, directing you on your journey. Remember every obstacle is a brick in your yellow brick road to success!!

This is why you have to listen to your intuition, that very thing deep inside of you telling you it's *'possible'* and you know that there is more to life than what you have been living. This is when the hero appears—you are now ready to discover the obstacles as you know they are showing you the way forward for something grander. If you see your obstacle as a doorway and not a block that is preventing you from living your truth, magic unfolds!

> *"If you're going to have a story, have a big story or none at all"* –
> **Joseph Campbell**.

Now that you are the hero of your story – if your story were up on a billboard, what would be the title of your movie?

Chapter 3
Honouring Your Own Boundaries...

"Walls keep everybody out. Boundaries teach them where the door is" – **Mark Groves**

In this chapter we are overcoming barriers, obstacles, and blocks to setting boundaries—a topic that is very personal and emotionally important to most of us. It's one that I still struggle with to this very day. And it isn't until you commit to the deep work that you start to realise how often you compromise your boundaries to please others.

I was your typical *'yes'* woman until I experienced burnout—more like a breakdown after eleven years of juggling motherhood and executive-hood. Something slowly seeped away from my sense of self. I felt as though I was living to exist as the *'good person'* in the lives of those around me. My real identity was rarely present, and my emotions were simply an afterthought or something I considered when I came home after an exhausting day.

It wasn't until I started working on my boundaries that I was able to identify why I was doing what I was doing in the first place. Was it to be appreciated or accepted? Was it to feel a sense of belonging? Was I a people-pleaser? Was I seeking something external to validate that I was in fact a good person? Or maybe it was an old-dated habit that no longer served me. Boundaries come in all shapes and sizes, and are at times, hard to identify.

Working through my lack of boundaries taught me many things. But more importantly, if someone throws a hissy fit because you set boundaries, well that's a sure sign the boundary was needed in the first place. One of my biggest lessons was that whatever you are willing to put up with is exactly what you will get. In other words, you get what you tolerate, and people will only do what you allow them to! Let that one marinate for a little while.

Boundaries are straightforward and easier to manage once you have well-defined values and areas of importance in your life.

You are only as good as your values…

Now that we have a little understanding of our values from the previous chapter, let's decide what exactly are our values. You have core values that never change no matter where you are in life and then there are other values that only serve in a particular chapter or area of your life. For example, what you may find important to you in your career, may not be the same as what is important to you in your life or relationships.

Values determine what we do with our time and how we evaluate the time that we have experienced. So, you may be thinking, then why is understanding values so important? When it comes to happiness, satisfaction, and bliss... understanding your values is a fundamental building block.

Your values influence your behaviours, choices, and emotions. Your values influence your habits, your lifestyle, and your social experiences. Your values are your motivators and provide a purpose for getting up and beginning your day.

Values determine your priorities, and they are probably the way you measure whether your life is turning out the way you want it to. When the things that you do and the way that you behave match your values, life is usually good right? You are satisfied and content. Somehow you feel successful, regardless of where you are at with other achievements such as career status.

But when these don't align with your values, that's when things feel—wrong. This can be a real source of unhappiness. Values exist, whether you recognise them or whether you are concerned with the idea of values or not. Life can be much easier when you acknowledge your values—when you make plans and decisions that honour them.

Love what you do and never work a day in your life...

Steve Jobs said – *"The only way to do great work is to love what you do. If you haven't found it yet, keep looking. Don't settle."* That's why it is super important to choose a job or career that you love, and you will never have to work a day in your life!

Generally speaking, we all have 24 hours in a day and most of us need at least 8 hours of sleep every night to feel fully rested. This leaves us with 16 hours left in our day. We invest 8 hours at work... then that leaves us with another 8 hours for *'me'* time. Have you ever pondered on how much time you invest at work? And whether that time energises you or do you walk away feeling depleted? This is how you measure whether you are aligned with your career values—you will run out of energy for things that are not important to you.

Think about this. Every Friday your energy slowly decreases after leaving work. You let out a sigh of relief for the weekend, reminding yourself that it will *'all be worth it'* once you push through. But what will all be worth it? What values are you living up to exactly?

Your energy and vibrational frequency will be at an all-time high when you are doing the things that light you up or the things that inspire and motivate you. For example, if you value family, but you must work a 70-hour week in your job, will you feel internal stress and conflict? And if you don't value competition, and you work in a highly competitive sales environment, are you likely to be satisfied with your job?

In these types of situations, understanding your values can really help. When you know your own values, you can use them to make decisions about how to live your life. If you have positivity as a core value but find yourself in a team of negative people at work, you might feel frustrated on the job, but not know why. Similarly, if you are in a high-pressure career and have a core value of peace you may find work draining, even if you have all the necessary skills and qualifications to get the job done.

True love has no endings...

What do you do when you fall out of love with your work? Yes. Out of love! You can either love or hate your work. There is a lot of research that shows that most individuals are not inspired by what they do but they do the job to pay the bills. If you look at what are the similarities between work and relationships, both are concerned with feeling connected and relating to one another. In other words, being the right fit.

Let's briefly discuss relationships. If you value intimacy and companionship, and they value their solitude, doing things their way, and no matter what they profess, they consistently do things that exclude you and make you feel anything but a companion, you are incompatible. The closer you get, the more they will move away. Even if they like a little intimacy, they only want it when they want it, which may be little. If you cannot manage this, it's not going to work. If they don't want to get closer, there is no point waiting around for them to potentially change.

If you say that you value love, care, trust, and respect, but you chase guys for passion, attraction, chemistry, and excitement, you'll likely end up with a fun-loving, great lay, that looks great and makes your heart skip, but treats you like a casual partner and has no desire to be in a committed relationship. Think about what you value and ask yourself why you value it.

Also, look at the values that you expect a partner to have—do you embody them? If not, why not?

- Why do you value money?
- Why do you value appearance?
- Why do you value success?
- Why do you value passion?

Then ask yourself, what do you believe these things will do for the relationship or for you? And what is the flip side of some of these things that you value? A classic example of this—the flip side to valuing appearance is that you are likely to be involved with superficial partners who don't value more substantial things about you. Or the alternative to valuing success is that if someone prioritises success, they may be totally focused on work and uninterested in a relationship or having a family.

The greatest wealth is health...

Some may value their health. If this is a strong value for you, then how do you feel the morning after a night out when you realise you have over-consumed alcohol and fast food? I'm pretty sure you would be feeling a strong sense of guilt, perhaps angry with yourself about your choice. You immediately get a sense that something is *'wrong'*. You're experiencing disharmony. This feeling would differ depending on how strongly you value your health because obviously, one night out isn't going to derail everyone's progress. When you experience disharmony between your values and your behaviour, unconsciously you will automatically take action to correct the situation and rectify your feelings.

If you value health and fitness and work crazy hours, have a family to look after and miss the gym that week, you may find yourself a little grumpy as you are not aligned with what is most important to you.

Therefore, staying true to your values is important because it navigates our direction. We can use our body compass by acknowledging what we are naturally moving towards without resistance or what we are moving away from.

Values are like fingerprints...

Values are those things that we judge as good or bad, right, or wrong, appropriate, or inappropriate. We also have highly valued criteria, which are our most important values and are very tied to our beliefs. Those are the convictions that we believe and trust as being true without a doubt.

Hold on to your values—don't compromise them. Your values are your guiding light. Your values are how you make your decisions. They are your unconscious drivers. They are your truth; they are what you believe in. The more you honour your values, the better you will feel about yourself and those you love. A trick is to stay in tune with your gut. Follow your gut feeling. If you feel resistance, ask yourself, *"why am I feeling this resistance?"* Don't just brush it off. You may just find your values have been compromised.

When you really unpack your triggers—it's often a compromise of your values system or beliefs. Values are what drive our thinking, feelings, attitudes, decisions, and behaviours. They are profoundly ingrained into the deeper part of our unconscious mind from the time we are born. Values are one-of-a-kind and exceptional to each one of us. They aren't just a random combination of positive descriptors we apply and interpret in specific ways.

Therefore, when we come across an individual that has opposing values, we will automatically feel agitated without really understanding why. Values are what we hold as sacred, important and are our foundation in all that we are, do or have.

Beliefs are many assumptions, hypotheses, and presumptions that we make about the world around us. Beliefs give us a sense of safety and a feeling of ease. Just like values, they are profoundly ingrained into that deeper part of the mind. Therefore, you can imagine how someone could absolutely lose their cool when there are conflicting thoughts, feelings and actions that are driven by values and beliefs.

In a nutshell, your beliefs are your *"I am"* statements and there are many but for the purpose of this exercise I will share some of my *"I am"* statements that affected every area of my life. *"I am not smart enough"*, *"I am not good enough"* and *"I am not worthy enough"* were on repeat, it's not to say they no longer exist but I am consciously aware of them now. Then get this, your *"I am"* statements then drive your values, the things that are important to you, which then impact the way you think, feel, and show up.

Your boundaries are not up for discussion...

> *"Emotional self-defence is an act of wisdom. Building personal boundaries is an act of strength. Anyone who tells you differently is often the reason we need both"* - **Steve Maraboli**.

Have you ever felt the overwhelm, deluged and inundation by the presence of another—no matter how much personal development you have indulged in? You realise that even if you had an endless supply of incense or sage sticks, you still feel uncomfortable after certain social situations. That my dearest is an indication that you must really take a good hard look at your boundaries.

Healthy boundaries are necessary components for self-care because without boundaries, we feel depleted, taken advantage of, taken for granted, intruded upon, or stepped over the top of as if we were a doormat. Whether our boundaries are crossed at work or in our personal relationships, poor boundaries may lead to resentment, hurt, anger, and burnout.

Although I find it uncomfortable saying *'no'* to others, setting boundaries helps others to understand what they can and can't do... they set a precedent. Boundaries are guidelines we set for ourselves, and they show others how they should behave appropriately in our company. Opinions and past personal histories often instigate boundaries, allowing us to feel physically, mentally, and spiritually safe. They involve beliefs, emotions, and self-esteem, operating during both incoming and outgoing interactions.

Setting boundaries doesn't make you mean...

Their purpose is to protect and care for ourselves. We must inform others when they're out of line. It's important to voice these feelings strongly because we're responsible for how we allow others to treat us. Boundaries can be defined as *'the limits we set with other people, which indicate what we find acceptable and unacceptable in their behaviour towards us'*.

The benefits that arise from setting healthy boundaries are endless, including maturity, assertiveness, less anger, and resentment because your needs are being met. The perquisite is that you feel safe, and at peace, incur increased confidence, improved communication, time, and energy to do things that nourish and bring joy to your body, mind, and spirit because you respect yourself and feel respected by others.

How many times have you thought to yourself – *"I've got this! My boundaries are solid as a rock!"* only to discover that every time you are around this one family member or co-worker you allow your boundaries to suddenly collapse, as though they never existed at all. Well... no one can make you feel anything unless you allow them to and nor can anyone take your power away from you unless you give away your power.

You get what you tolerate...

> *"The difference between successful people and really successful people is that really successful people say no to almost everything"* — **Warren Buffet**.

Boundaries. Boundaries. Boundaries. Now that we have an understanding of what they are and how we create them because after all, they are unique to you. They are the limits and rules that you set for yourself. And boundaries can be physical, emotional, and intellectual. You can set firm boundaries within relationships, your energy, and your time.

Boundaries grant you access to get more of what you want and less of what you don't want. A person with healthy boundaries can say *'no'* to others whenever they want to, without feeling guilty. They protect and honour the space that they have created to clarify what behaviours are acceptable and unacceptable from others.

What you allow is what will continue. Most of us want to do the right thing. We make it our job to fix others or feel the need to take responsibility for others. We get real joy out of seeing others happy. It's not our job to make others happy. It's not our job to make sure everyone is feeling good. And it's not our job to fix problems that don't belong to us.

Effective human beings have boundaries. As a result, they can see that it allows others to grow because they become more conscious of their own behaviours. Boundaries keep us in control of time, energy, and safety. It's a way of looking after yourself. It's almost a duty for us to have boundaries. Otherwise, people will take advantage of you and walk all over you.

The benefits are endless. Not only are you contributing to others' well-being, but you are also walking your talk and taking care of yourself. This, my dearest, is how you build more respect from others and more self-respect.

A lack of boundaries invites a lack of respect...

Where does a lack of boundaries come from? It's hereditary. The beautiful Terri Cole, a renowned psychotherapist, explains that when you were growing up if you were not allowed to close your bedroom or bathroom doors or have a private conversation on the phone with a friend, it would have an impact on your boundaries today.

If you were encouraged or discouraged to express your individual feelings, especially if they differed from the majority and if you were allowed to differentiate from them, that too would affect your boundaries.

In addition, if it was a family system where everyone knew what was going on in your life, whether you wanted them to know or not, it would influence the way you form or do not form your boundaries today as an adult.

Terri also mentions that if there was one person in your family who was more controlling than everyone else. For example, a very domineering mother or father—that too is where your boundaries come from. The same goes for a dominating sibling, especially if they were an addict in some way and you had to sublimate your own desires and wishes because there was a greater problem to be solved.

Boundaries come from having a good sense of self-worth...

Another reason for a lack of boundaries is if you had uninvolved or negligent parents, and not always intentionally so. For example, when my parents came to Australia from France to start all over again, they were never home, but they worked damn hard to make ends meet. Consequently, it meant I had to grow up fast.

In most situations when we are young, our feelings are heavily influenced by how others feel about us and treat us—especially our parents. When you don't get the guidance and attention you need, it can cause significant self-esteem problems. This also ties in with whether your parents were non-vocal, verbal, or physical when working through problems.

Growing up in an environment where you weren't respected can make you feel like something is wrong with you. If you were pressured to do things you were not comfortable with and your thoughts and feelings weren't valued, you may end up feeling that the only way for you to be liked is to do what others want, not what you need.

The key is not to prioritise what's on your schedule but to schedule your priorities.

Prioritise your needs. In doing so, if people get upset about you setting boundaries, they are the ones who were benefiting from you having none in the first place.

It's never too late to regain your respect. You can start setting boundaries with a few simple yet highly effective steps:

1. Cultivate awareness and articulate what you need to change. What specific boundaries have been violated or ignored?
2. Identify the unhealthy thinking and beliefs by which you allow your boundaries to be violated.

3. Create a new belief that will encourage you to change your behaviours so that you build healthy boundaries between yourself and others.
4. In turn, you will gain insight into what new behaviours you need to add to your healthy boundary so that your space, privacy, and rights are no longer violated.
5. Awareness, change, and growth are necessary for you to build strong boundaries. It is up to you to decide how you respond to others.

Remember. Setting clear, firm boundaries means that you don't automatically react to everyone's thoughts and feelings. You tolerate other opinions and do not become defensive when you disagree. You recognise that your reaction is your responsibility. You say *'no'* with comfort and ease. It's time to say goodbye to abusive behaviours. What boundaries will you set today?

Everything you are going through is just preparation…

Guess what? I have a little, magical life lesson to share with you. YOU are the creator of your own reality. No one else can create your life for you … it's yours to do all on your own! I'm pretty sure you have guessed that by now reading over the chapters.

When you step into this very powerful belief that you are the creator or manifesto of everything in your environment, it becomes a very empowering standpoint. It's that point in life where you realise that if you can make it, you can change it.

Your beliefs, thoughts and emotions all come back as the world around you. Your external world experiences are simply a mirror of yourself and the energy that emanates. It reflects what you think, feel, and believe, it will expose you to how you operate. If only you would just stop, put the phone down and actually take notice.

Everything you are going through is just preparation. If you are annoyed with something or someone, suddenly what you see is that other people who act '*annoyed*' or are '*annoying*' will pop into your focus.

If you don't respect yourself then others won't respect, you. If you don't believe you are worthy of a pay increase, or a promotion then guess what? Others will see you exactly that way. If you are careless and you don't look after people or objects as if it was your own, then you will receive exactly that. Others will be careless with you and your belongings.

Stop asking why they keep doing it and start asking why you keep allowing it…

That is indeed a hard pill to swallow because you have nowhere else to go. You are undoubtedly in charge of yourself. No more blaming, judging or criticising. The moment you can take full responsibility for what is going on in your life—it becomes a game changer. Not only is it empowering but there will be a sense of freedom like you've never felt before.

Now to take accountability one step further we must take a good hard look at the violations of our internal boundaries. These may include those promises that you make to yourself, whether it's being more persistent with your goals, breaking commitments or keeping secrets. Internal boundaries are between you and you. Yep. These boundaries assist you to coordinate, adjust and balance the relationship you have with yourself!

Then there are external boundaries such as time boundaries, including how much time you spend with someone, doing something for someone or how much time you invest at work.

Another boundary type is conversational, which involves topics that you are open to discussing and not discussing. We then have content boundaries, which are things that you will and not will consume such as social media, news, or television. Finally, there are personal boundaries you have placed with yourself based on your own unique needs.

People-pleasing is keeping you trapped...

How often have you said *"yes"* to something and two seconds later, kicked yourself for it? Saying *"yes"* when you really want to say *"no"* is a clear indication that there may be some sneaky people-pleasing tendencies. Don't you ever wonder why we do such things? Well in my research I have found a plethora of lists for you to digest, and it could be a number of reasons such as.

- Fear of letting others down or disappointing them
- Afraid of losing people in fear they may leave you
- Avoiding any form of conflict, not wanting to rock the boat
- Fear of rejection and disappointing others
- Your self-worth comes from external validation
- You want to fit in, connect with others and belong
- You don't want to feel guilty for saying *"no"*
- You lack self-love and self-worth
- You want others to like you and be nice to you

There are many more where they came from, however, from my work thus far these seem to be the most relevant ones and the ones that I see play out often with my clients.

Sometimes you don't realise you are actually drowning when you are trying to be everyone else's anchor. If you want to live a life full of purpose, you need to start saying *"no"* and be okay with it. It might not make people happy, but it will be freeing to know you are not responsible for everyone's happiness. You should not be afraid to lose people. Instead, you should be afraid of losing yourself by trying to please everyone around you.

Your life isn't yours if you constantly care what others think...

The secret to saying *"no"* ... If you've ever invested any time with a toddler, you'll notice that they say *"no"* a lot. In developmental terms, this is a big milestone, and it happens around the age of 2-3 years. A recent study found that toddlers argue with their parents as often as 20-25 times per hour! The important fact here is that toddlers are not doing this to be difficult and defy parental authority. For them, it's more about exerting a sense of self and a sense of control to make their little world a bit less overwhelming.

Adults can learn a thing or two from this. Relocating this sense of self is a good start. Saying *"no"* is hard. You don't want to be seen as rude, difficult, or unhelpful. So don't give people reason to think that at all. Smile, and politely say one of these alternatives:

- Can I get back to you?
- Can I think about it?
- Unfortunately, it's not a good time right now
- Maybe another time
- Sounds great, but I have other commitments
- Could you please give me more information before I decide?
- Thank you, but no thank you
- I'd love to, but I can't
- Thank you for thinking of me, but I can't
- Another time might be better
- I'm not sure if I am the best person for it
- I'm trying to cut back on commitments
- I won't be able to dedicate the extra time needed for this project

Saying *"no"* may be daunting at times but the more you do it, the easier the process becomes. As a result, the benefits will help you with self-care, building your self-esteem and confidence. This is because you are choosing where you invest your time and energy by allowing you to focus on giving it to the people and parts of your life that really deserve it. And this is when we'll start to thrive.

Obstacles show you the way forward...

> *"If you can find a path with no obstacles, it probably doesn't lead anywhere"* – **Frank Clark**.

Obstacles are an interesting concept. Obstacles are inevitable. And to be honest, unless you're a psychic you'll never be able to accurately predict when they're going to pop up, or what's going to pan out as a result. Obstacles are ALWAYS surprises.

Sometimes they're good surprises, sometimes they're challenging surprises. Imagine just for a moment that you're driving to the countryside this weekend. Lots of things could take shape; it could start to rain or snow. You might pop a tyre or one of your children could get carsick ... because sh!t happens. And we have no control over the obstacles that arise.

What we do have control over, is how we react and respond to these obstacles. We can choose to get flustered and stressed and waste energy lamenting that *'this was not part of the plan!'* Or we can use our energy positively to learn and move forward.

Obstacles are usually accompanied by negative emotions—fear, worry, stress, anxiety, you get the general idea ... and for this very reason, they are also an opportunity to grow and expand.

I'm not saying that you don't deserve to get a bit angry or annoyed as you're sitting by the roadside in the rain waiting for a tyre change ... but later, when you're calm and reflective, obstacles can provide a vital opportunity to look at the way we handle things. They help us determine what buttons within us get *'pushed'* and how we react in certain situations.

Uncertainty is a fact of life. If we all knew what was going to happen next, then the journey wouldn't be half as much fun! But uncertainty, or the tough times you may be going through, whether on a personal or on a professional level can be stressful and sometimes it's important to recognise that we need a helping hand.

A problem often leads to opportunities because they challenge us...

When you think about it, life is one big obstacle course. It constantly forces you to meet new challenges that you must try to overcome in order to avoid being stuck in a fixed mindset...

Challenges are extremely important for one's life for many reasons—essentially, they unveil your true potential, and your willpower to keep moving forward and they help reveal your identity. They show who you become during these turbulent times and what you are capable of. You know that saying *"what doesn't kill you, makes you stronger!"* If anything, challenges make you tougher and more resilient.

Like all things in life, it is the meaning we give to every circumstance, and I do mean every situation! For example, when something doesn't go according to plan, you can either wallow and go down the rabbit hole of *'why'* me and be the victim of circumstance. Or... you can look at the situation and identify where you went wrong, what you learned from it and what you are going to do differently next time.

You see, it is up to us as to what meaning we apply to wanted or unwanted emotions. It is up to us how we interpret and give our experiences meaning. If anything, obstacles direct your actions, they show you the way forward, and they let you know if you are going in the right direction or if you have hit a dead end. They direct you on your path and enable you to focus on what truly counts but most importantly, obstacles unleash your creativity.

7 Ways to conquer any kind of obstacle...

Nothing is impossible. When you break it down, the word itself says *'I'm possible'*. What would your world look like if there were no problems and only opportunities?

1) Mindset is everything.

Mindset is everything in driving your success. We all have a choice as to what we include in our reality. It is that easy. This is now a habit. Such a mindset is my default position, which means that every time something happens, I look at the opportunity at hand rather than get stuck in the problem. Mind you, it took me time to perfect it. Our friend Napoleon Hill says it perfectly – *"Every adversity, every failure, every heartache carries with it the seed of an equal or greater benefit."* This really resonates with me; every time I am faced with a problem, I ask myself: what is the opportunity here?

Going back twenty years ago, I did some work with a large corporation, and they were on the market for sale. This is what happened as soon as it was announced. Most of the people—up to 90% were—so focused on the sale as a negative situation rather than a positive one. The gossip went up to double in almost a week. Fear was out of control. People were running around, stressing out of their brains whether they still had a job after the sale. Productivity dropped immensely. Individuals were concerned about their security. There was so much uncertainty, which created even more havoc.

In reality, when a group undergoes change and uncertainty, it is not the organisation that changes, but the behaviours of the individuals. That's right. It is the meaning we give any situation as our reality. If only we were conscious enough to pause and shift our mindset, moving away from the problematic way of thinking to opportunities like this. This means I will:

- Get a promotion
- Be rewarded with a pay increase
- Work with a new kick-ass boss
- Do what I love and use my talents
- Work in a different department
- Relocate, the drive to work may be shorter

In times of change, we can experience self-realisation or an *'aha'* moment. Maybe we didn't even realise that our potential is stronger somewhere else. Shifting our mindset to what the opportunities at hand are will create movement. It will loosen the boundaries of the problem; it will open up your thinking to discover that anything is possible.

2) **Endure in the possible.**

With the right attitude, hard work and perseverance, you will create a reality of possibilities. And without a structure in place to execute a plan, great possibilities simply become wishful thinking. The problem lies with our beliefs, perceptions, and assumptions that we hold to be true. A problem may initially feel impossible until you engage with it.

There are many individuals who look for any reason as to why something is not possible, and guess what? They get really creative in circulating excuses, to find reasons as to why nothing besides negativity will work for them. Progress can only happen if we open our mindset to the possibility of a different and better way. We can train our minds to move from impossible to possible. If there is no evidence or past experience of this problem, then it is fear-based. It is a figment of your imagination, and it is not real.

In actual fact, it is your mind making up excuses and not taking responsibility for what is really going on. Making up excuses leaves no room for improvement. It is quite debilitating and disempowering. If your outlook is to think it's impossible, you are saying it's possible for someone else. It keeps you stuck with the problem. However, if you were in a place of accountability and owned your reality, there is so much more room for you to move with. It's no longer a matter of who can make it possible. It's more of a matter of how you can make it possible. So much more empowering, don't you think?

We so often advocate or condone our positions by offering an alternative person, time, and place. This takes a load of responsibility off our shoulders and places it onto another. However, if you were to think only you could do this task, you are now in business to think everything is an opportunity. Remember, we were all born with endless possibilities and potential.

3) What else could this mean?

We frequently get caught up in gossip or problems. The uncertainty overwhelms us. But... What if we were to embrace uncertainty and chaos? What would your world look like then? My favourite probing question to loosen the boundaries of any problem is to look at the multi-facets of the problem with one simple question – *'what else could this mean?'* I then proceed to write a mammoth list of all the different possibilities of that problem.

To conquer any obstacles or embrace uncertainty, there has to be a level of acceptance. Accept things as they are. It could be as simple as this is happening right now. How much control do I have over the outcome? 90% of the time we have zero control over it. So why not invest your time and energy in the things that you can control? Acceptance has movement; it can shift you from feeling happy to being happy. I also believe finding the purpose and the lesson behind every challenge will assist you to embrace whatever is going on for you. And acceptance doesn't mean settling for less, but rather knowing there is more than one way to be happy and get what you want.

4) Keep moving forward.

Keep moving. Keep busy. Create goals that you have control over and have checkpoints or milestones so that you can tick them off one by one to create momentum. For example, I will set myself a particular goal, which has an end date of three months. Every month I think: *"what is the one thing I want to achieve this month that will contribute to my end goal?"* Then I break it down into four small action points to be completed each week. It creates movement and momentum; you can see you are moving towards your end goal. One step at a time. Slow and steady wins the race.

5) Believe you can create anything.

We have the incredible power of imagination and belief. If you believe you can, you will. The same rule applies if you believe you can't. Every idea and triumph that every individual has ever created was the innovation of their imagination. Everything and all experiences have their starting point in the imagination. When you harness the power of your imagination and make it an integral part of your activity of love and life, then wonderful things start to manifest. It's magical.

There is great power in believing that something is possible. Imagination is a powerful force. It brings things that did not exist before into the realm of possibility. To manifest our imagination into the real world, the most important ingredient is a deep sense of belief in our work and our abilities.

6) No expectations. No disappointments.

Replace expectations with plans. To do that is to control the controllable. Once you have worked out what is in your control, you can easily prepare a different plan towards possibility. If you are only doing what is barely possible, you are most likely staying in your comfort zone.

For most of us, the conversion from doing what is necessary to what is possible will lead to what you once thought impossible, into achievable. The best plan is to start with small steps into the zone of necessity and then into possibility. When you see yourself achieving small victories, you are telling your belief system that it is possible. Tiny steps all add up to a huge leap.

7) Become an observer of your story.

Can you disassociate yourself from your story? Great. Can you now become the observer of the story instead of being in the story? If you remain associated with your limiting belief or limiting decision, then you won't have much success in moving towards possibility. However, if you disassociate yourself from the story, you can see it from a different perspective. You can separate yourself from the problem. Then this makes the problem tangible and something you can work with.

Give it a go! It is completely up to you. The meaning you give any scenario is your complete choice.

You playing small doesn't serve the world...

It is our light, not our darkness, that most frightens us. Our deepest fear is not that we are inadequate. Our deepest fear is that we are powerful beyond measure.

And the thing about that is, whatever we reject from our *'self'* comes back to us in our world as an event or situation. Why? So, we can learn from it. Some of us see the lesson for the first time, others take it numerous times. Always remember we're each on our own personal journey, so it is not a competition. The important thing to know is that we don't become enlightened by imagining the light around us. We become enlightened by looking at our dark side. Unless you learn to face your own shadows, you will continue to see them in others, because the world outside of you is only a reflection of the world inside you.

When you know your worth, no one can make you feel useless. Today is your time, and not another minute should be wasted because tomorrow may be a missed opportunity. By now you are starting to get the idea that personal boundaries have everything to do with how you show up. This is because they are drawn from the framework of your core beliefs, perspective, opinions of yourself and values.

In what areas of life are you holding back and playing small? Think about the times you consistently feel weak or small, or the times you find decision-making a real challenge, or when you really dislike letting other people down. Try to put a face and name to the part of you that feels disempowered.

- What does it look like or sound like?
- How old is it and where did it come from?
- What name would it choose to call itself?

By personifying this afraid and suppressed part of you, you'll be more capable of understanding an important part of your shadow self.

Guilt and anxiety, the terrible twins...

If you have ever experienced guilt or anxiety—or both, there is a correlation between a lack of boundaries and not having your needs met. A lack of boundaries goes back as far as your childhood, where you may have experienced a caregiver who didn't provide unconditional love and acceptance. You always had to do what others wanted to as a way of avoiding being rejected or abandoned. And... Now as an adult those are the two things you fear the most.

Boundaries are very evident when it comes to family, first and foremost. How often have you said, *"yes"* because you felt guilty if you said *"no"* only to be feeling a little annoyed because you didn't stand in your truth?

Our siblings are powerful mirrors that reflect back on our own undeveloped talents, rejected personality traits, and shadow qualities. If you have siblings, take some time to think about them and see what your relationship is like with them. In what ways do they irritate, provoke, disappoint, or otherwise hurt you? Afterwards, look for any lessons that may be buried beneath your reflections. Are there any specific qualities or traits you might be denying within yourself and projecting onto your sibling(s)? What shadows does the behaviour of your brother or sister provoke within you?

You can also do this with your parents, guardians, or family members. What qualities in your family members do you most dislike or have trouble dealing with? What might these qualities secretly reveal about you? Don't hold back, allow yourself to write it all down with no judgement, where you can stand in your truth. This is for your eyes only, no one needs to see it but you.

It takes two to tango no matter what...

Once you start doing the shadow work, don't be surprised if most of the time, they are associated with your direct connections such as family, friends, and partnerships, which is one of the biggest lessons that I have experienced thus far.

Whenever you experience envy and jealousy or find yourself criticising and judging, these are sure signs that you have some serious shadow work to get started on. This is where the deep work begins. You must identify what personality qualities or traits you envy or that you wish you had, or simply developing awareness of these triggers will help you reveal a hidden shadow gift.

There is no need to be beating yourself up about such thoughts because everyone has an inner judge... It is a necessity or a fundamental part of life. Without the inner judge, we would make poor decisions, live disconnected from reality, and be incapable of self-reflection. But when the inner judge is too prominent in our lives, our minds are filled with harsh and critical self-talk and the impulse to condemn others. The inner judge is a major cause of low self-esteem and is fuelled by negative core beliefs and distorted thoughts.

When you catch yourself judging, just ask *"in what areas of my life do I exhibit the exact same behaviours as those I judge?"* Just wait and see what bubbles up for you. In our previous chapter, we did a little dive into judgement and self-judgement. Non-judgement just means that you don't need to do something about every single life experience.

Our lives are a perfect reflection of our beliefs...

Indeed, our beliefs are ingrained within us. Their roots are deep. But we have the power to break unhealthy patterns and retrain our brains. It just takes a little awareness and action. As humans, we tend to think that our beliefs are based on reality. However, beliefs are delusions. Assumptions. They are not real. known or not known.

We have come to understand that it is our unconscious mind that creates our reality. It runs the show when we are not being *'present'* and *'mindful'* in our own lives. We have also come to learn that our beliefs govern our experiences. The beliefs that we hold to be true, precious, and important become our identity, reflecting who we are and how we live our lives. Life responds to demand. In order to demand, we have to know what we want. Otherwise, life will draw us to all the things that are associated with our beliefs. This is how we create our lives.

When working with self-beliefs, take a moment and explore something that is really upsetting or frustrating you. Ask yourself why you are feeling what you are feeling and then keep asking the question *'why'* until you run out of answers. There my friend is where you will find the root cause of your belief. Let me bring it to life with an example. I feel like nobody likes me. Why? Because no one ever asks me to go out with them. Why? Because I say *"no"* most of the time when asked to catch up with people. Why? Because I prefer to be alone. Why? Because I don't think I have anything intelligent to say. Why? Because I don't think I am worthy of attention. And there it is my friend! The moment you have an *"I am"* statement this is your belief right there.

Self-confidence is the foundation of all great success...

Self-confidence is important in almost every aspect of our lives, yet many people struggle to find it. Let me ask you this: how would you feel with more confidence? What would you be doing that you are not currently doing? How different would your life look right now? In what situations do you most lack confidence?

There is so much research now that tells us that the more confident individuals, leaders, entrepreneurs, and business owners are, the more successful their achievements and the happier they are in their personal and professional life. And the one trait they have in common is this: Setting a small goal, a totally achievable one – which moves them forward, steadily, one step at a time.

Each and every one of us is capable of building confidence. There isn't a one-set rule on how to raise your self-confidence—your path towards it will be as unique as you are. Carol Dweck sends a very strong message when she says that if parents want to give their children a gift, the best thing they can do is to teach their children to love challenges, be intrigued by mistakes, enjoy effort, and keep on learning. That way, their children don't have to be slaves of praise. They will have a lifelong skill – the ability to build and repair their own confidence. In essence, they'll have resilience, no matter what comes their way.

Raising your own confidence is about trying something new, without the *'fear'* of making a mistake because there is NO FAILURE ... only feedback! When we make mistakes and we actually learn to embrace them, then we open ourselves to the possibility of learning. When we learn, we grow and build deeper confidence.

Fear is a state of mind…

Remember what you resist will persist. So, if you resist the fear, it will just get stronger. The antidote is to be aware of it when it arises. You can do so by practising daily mindfulness, which is just about being present with your thoughts. Become aware of what is unfolding before your eyes. Be willing to dance with your fear as it emerges. Observe what you are thinking at that very moment.

The intention is not to eradicate your fear. The aim is to change the way you associate yourself with fear. Once you accept the fear, it no longer has power over you. Recognising, acknowledging, and appreciating the presence of fear will allow you to make a conscious decision. You choose to have faith and accept the fear. As a result, you have the assurance that it is giving you clarity over what the fear is guiding you to do ... or even what it is stopping you from doing.

Remember, the choice is yours. Fear is not a foe, a villain, or an attacker. It can be the voice of reasoning, foresight and attention that serves you adequately, smoothly, and successfully at times. Resisting fear takes up way too much of your time, energy, and creativity. Accept it for what it is. Admit its very existence. Only then can you experience the wonder that comes with embracing fear through faith. What do you fear losing the most?

Money block fears...

When it comes to fear—it comes in different forms, shapes, and sizes. And when we speak of obstacles, blocks, and barriers, they too can come in many different areas of our life. One fear that we can all relate to is money blocks.

Money is energy. It is a means of exchange for your goods or services as an exchange for the energy that you put into your work to receive money. In saying that some of us have unconscious money blocks that we are not even aware of... money blocks are what is stopping you from getting what you want!

What are money blocks? Some of the money blocks that I have encountered are:

Self-worth – *Receiving money* – some of us feel uncomfortable receiving money; especially if we are people-pleasers. If money is energy and you give all your energy away and are not seeing to your own needs first, then what kind of message are you sending out to the Universe? Exactly! You will manifest money for others, so you may find yourself working hard to fulfil others' needs and be left feeling tired and burned out all the time.

Self-sabotage – *Having money* – some of us feel uncomfortable about having money, so we spend it. Buy things that you don't need and then you never have money left over, regardless of how much money you're making, you spend excessively! This leads to feeling insecure about money and not saving money!

Self-evaluation – *Comparison* – some of us just can't help but compare our situation to someone else. This can become a perpetuating effect, leaving you powerless and feeling unhappy because you are always seeking externally from others. It can have a massive impact on your self-worth and when you don't feel worthy, energetically it has an impact on your financial worth.

Perception – *Beliefs* – stories about money; it could be as simple as your parents telling you money doesn't grow on trees or maybe you experience your parents fighting about money, so now you think money is evil. This kind of money block is related to negative emotions such as shame, fear, grief, guilt, or anger, which are all unconscious of course. The only way to become aware of your money blocks is by working through the process that we are about to embark on.

If you were to explore the shadows lurking underneath your relationship with money, what is standing out for you right now? How do you respond to money when you lack or have lots of money? What triggers feelings of shame, guilt, anxiety, or any general discomfort? One thing to keep in mind is, money is not evil, it is simply a symbolic medium of exchange, instead, it is our relationship with money that is the issue.

Chapter 4
Building True Confidence, Impostor Syndrome, Ego and the Fear of Not Being Good Enough...

"Nothing can harm you as much as your own thoughts unguarded" – **Buddha**

Being confident has nothing to do with how *'perfect'* you are—it has nothing to do with how superior you are to anyone or anything. Confidence is about tapping into your inner courage and not letting fear or comparison with others hold you back. And it is not something we grab a hold of and never let go of, it comes, and it goes in its own rhythm.

Cultivating confidence doesn't mean never experiencing fear. Instead, it means that you feel the fear but continue anyway.

You may be confident in one area of your life but in the same breath lack confidence in another area of your life. For example, a singer may be confident performing in front of family and friends but may have crippling stage fright if the opportunity to sing in front of the public were to arise. When I think about it really, it's simply me getting in the way of me! We all do it, we all allow our fears to get in our own way and our own potential.

We get in our way by placing judgement on ourselves with the voice of our inner critic. *"I will fail," "It will be a disaster," "I don't have it in me," "I'm not good enough," "People will reject me,"* and the list goes on. For as long as we continue to play that repeating mantra in our mind, our reticular activating system (RAS) will find evidence to prove our doubts are correct.

RAS operates similar to a filter between the two parts of the brain—the conscious mind and the unconscious mind. It takes instructions from your conscious mind and sends them to your unconscious mind. A perfect example is when you're considering buying a new car. You have a particular budget in mind but can't help but fantasise about what it would be like to have that Mustang you have been dreaming about since you were a kid. Then all of a sudden, everywhere you go, you find yourself constantly pointing out that car to your partner because it keeps popping up everywhere you turn.

This is your RAS at work. It's a clever automatic mechanism inside your brain that brings relevant information to your attention. It's a little bit like a radar ... and it gravitates your focus to things you're captivated by and curious about.

Remember that confidence is a capacity that is available to everyone. You won't be completely confident overnight—but through time and persistence, you will strengthen this skill. Just don't forget to show love towards your frailties, self-love is a great doorway to more confidence. And it's an even grander entry when we practise it even during those times when it's the last thing, we feel like doing.

In the pursuit of perfectionism...

Perfectionism can be a confidence killer. Yep. You heard right. I have worked with so many perfectionists over the years and as with all things, it is wonderfully simple to dish out good and proven advice, however, it is a whole other kettle of fish to dish it up on your own plate.

Here's the thing...perfectionism has its merits, a job well done is never a negative thing, after all, nonetheless, where does it come from? If you, like me, are a self-professed perfectionist, have you ever actually wondered or tried to pinpoint its place of birth in your life?

Neuroscience and psychology, along with ancient teachings from esoteric modalities, put forth a dagger-to-the-heart realisation for every proud perfectionist... perfectionism is based on unworthiness.

Upon first conceptualising this, it can be almost sad that it was not more obvious, to begin with. Of course, feeling unworthy would push a person to deliver above and beyond the average. As expected, feelings of inadequacy would cause a person to furiously prove otherwise. Isn't that a good thing though, I hear you ask. Surely if one feels unworthy and pushes themselves to be better, that is far more admirable than not doing anything about it at all.

Perfectly imperfect...

There is a saying... It's not what you know or what you know you don't know, it's what you don't know that you don't know, that's what gets you! It's a mouthful that basically means we can't work with something we have no knowledge of. There are two sides to the coin of each tendency, of each feeling, of each pattern of behaviour we emit just because that's *'who we are'*. The flip side of perfectionism is that you feel you have something to prove; that you don't already feel worthy within your own skin.

We all know perfection is impossible and that it is found only in imperfection in reality. So why try so hard? Too hard? It is okay to miss a full stop here or there, to make errors, to even embarrass yourself—these are the limbs of the trees that if you are daring enough to climb out on, bear you fruit.

Going out on these limbs, and opening up to allowing yourself to be imperfect will teach you more about who you are and who you can be than the box of fear that tells you that you are less than others because you are flawed. Fear isn't real, of course, you are flawed, we all are, and we cannot ever find love, no compassion or empathy, or give ourselves room to grow and change if we are stuck within a box of limitations.

Remember when you were younger and had to follow unproductive rules that really had no purpose? A good example is being told you do not have permission to use the bathroom in school.

Every time you questioned the reason behind this rule, you were hit with *"because it's the rules!"* Which of course doesn't make sense. Rules are meant to benefit society as a whole and it is unclear how not using the bathroom is helpful to anyone. So how would you say being a perfectionist and stressing yourself out over every minor detail is beneficial? Especially when it's costing your happiness and when the task can actually be done better without the pointless panic and self-hatred.

Dare to both think and live outside the box and you might just find you feel more worthy than you ever did stressing over minor disasters and mini catastrophes!

Procrastination is a classic perfectionism ploy...

> *"Perfection consists not in doing extraordinary things, but in doing ordinary things extraordinarily well"* –
> **Angelique Arnauld**.

There is nothing wrong with striving to do the best you can, right? Absolutely nothing. But when you strive for perfection all the time, in everything that you do, you could be causing yourself some unnecessary heartache.

Recent studies have shown that perfectionist attitudes actually interfere with success. Self-defeating thoughts and behaviours are associated with being a *'perfectionist'*. Setting high and unrealistic goals can mean that perfectionists put themselves under constant, ridiculous amounts of pressure because of the expectations they have of what they can achieve. The desire to be perfect can deny you a sense of satisfaction and cause you to actually achieve far less than people with more realistic goals.

If you're a perfectionist reading this, I know what your brain may be telling you. That nobody understands how you're feeling because they don't hold themselves to the same high standards as you. And what would the researchers know, perhaps they weren't trying hard enough themselves. I understand it's hard to control these thoughts. But if you can hold onto them for a moment, I promise this chapter will encourage you to think otherwise.

So as for the idea of perfectionism achieving you less, it isn't really all it's cracked up to be. A sense of accomplishment and a sense of pride in what you're doing are both admirable, healthy attitudes, but when perfection kills your passion, then you're on the wrong track.

It's important to know your limitations because when they're your primary driver, perfectionism can get in your way of launching a project or finishing an assignment because *'it just doesn't look right'*. It can be an unnecessary burden that takes the fun out of things, and it can also powerfully influence the way we feel about ourselves.

Perfectionism reduces playfulness...

Do you know why you strive for excellence? It is most likely that you learned early on in life that you were mainly valued for your achievements. As a result, you may have learned to value yourself on the basis of other people's approval. So, your self-esteem may be based primarily on external standards. This can leave you vulnerable and sensitive to the opinions and criticism of others.

Perfectionism is often associated with fear of failure, making mistakes, or protecting oneself from critique, rejection, and disapproval. Perfectionists frequently believe that they are worthless; therefore, they need to keep proving themselves. Perfectionists also tend to see others as achieving success with a minimum of effort, few errors, little emotional stress, and maximum self-confidence. At the same time, perfectionists view their own efforts as an unending sense of duty and forever inadequate.

Perfectionism is an illusion...

This premise is very similar to the disease of busyness that we're currently experiencing across our society. People seem to place a lot of value on how *'busy'* they are when in reality it should be the other way around because this is a trap within itself. If you believe your self-worth is based on how *'busy'* you are, then you may find yourself never having any downtime and not having enough time to enjoy life.

Imagine if we lived in a society that highly valued those people who have a healthy balance, a life which proportions work, relaxation, time to recharge, exercise, and with family and friends. Imagine if this was the determinant of a *'successful'* life and not the hours you clock up at the office, the salary you bring home, where you live, what you drive and how many gadgets you own, or the fact that you never have free time to just do ... well, nothing, if that's what you want.

Overcoming perfectionism...

The first step is to understand what drives your perfectionism. Then challenge those self-defeating thoughts and behaviours and decide within yourself that you want to change. Stop. Review. Set new goals that are more realistic and achievable. Set goals with a plan and milestones along the way that you can feel good about achieving. Celebrate the wins, learn from the losses, and remind yourself often that sometimes, under some circumstances *'done and getting a good night's sleep, is better than perfect'*.

By focusing on the process and not the end result, you become mindful.... And this allows you to check in with how you feel about what you're doing. Are you enjoying it? If you are, great! Keep going. If you are not, explore that too... it's always important to understand what motivates you, and if you discover that it's fear ... fear of failure, then just smile at yourself. A lot of perfectionists are actually afraid of failure. But there is a world where failure doesn't exist, only feedback, and that might be something you want to investigate next.

To make a mistake is human...

Making mistakes is a critical part of evolving as a human being; if you make one, embrace it. And ask yourself "What did I just learn?" Pursuing excellence and having high standards is nothing to be ashamed of, it means you care, and you are putting in a lot of time, energy, and effort. You are not afraid to challenge the status quo and you get pleasure out of achieving what others can't do, just beware of the flip side and taking it too far... just saying.

Perfectionism can mean that you've set unrelenting standards, or that you blame yourself when things go wrong, or that in your mind no achievement is ever *'enough'* ... there goes that word again *'not good enough'* and having no faith that others will do something well enough, and you become a control freak that no one wants to be around (*including yourself*).

You are more than extraordinary, and you know you can put in a big effort when you need to and rely on yourself to get the task done well. Remind yourself of this every time you feel your need for perfectionism getting out of control. The most important thing of all is that you're enjoying your accomplishment. Not just the end result, but also the journey along the way.

The advantage of persisting self-doubt...

We have all heard of it before! Fear and self-doubt are the greatest killers of personal genius ... but are they really? What does self-doubt mean to you personally? Self-doubt can mean a lack of confidence, a lack of one's ability, or a lack of faith. It can indicate fear of criticism, fear of judgement, or fear of making the wrong decision.

In the same breath ... self-doubt can also suggest the desire to express your needs or to believe in yourself and back your ideas. Maybe it is asking you to get real with your feelings, whether it has something to do with your work, relationships, or money.

It's the meaning we give it! Whatever it means to you, it is asking you to *'stop'* and *'think'* because this little apprehension is trying to tell you something and thus one needs to investigate the trepidation, the uncertainty, and the hesitation of you moving forward.

This, by the way, is how you stay unstuck from self-doubt. By going in with a curious mindset and with the intention to figure out what it's trying to tell you, instead of accepting it for what it is. Trust your self-doubt, your little nudges, hunches, inklings, and feelings ... This is your intuitive intelligence speaking to you and asking you to slow down and listen.

Don't let self-doubt hold you back...

Self-doubt is not who you are, it's acting as an illusion ... a barrier that blocks you from going any further. It is inviting you to reassess, re-examine, review, and revise your thoughts, feelings, and decisions. Self-doubt is an opportunity to re-evaluate what you want...

What if you saw self-doubt as a bright light illuminating your blind spots? Or as a magic clock providing you with an extra moment to review what you're doing?

What if self-doubt was a way to bring all your unconscious programs and patterns into the conscious part of your mind to explore ... as a way to give you the ability to change the program. What about if you looked at self-doubt as a skill, intelligence, logical and emotionally essential? What then?

When you start to question your self-doubt, it gives you space to challenge and shift your perceptions ... thus bringing awareness to the opportunities and possibilities that self-doubt can bring to your consciousness and at the same time giving you an option to change course.

Thought-provoking questions opens your curious mind, it creates agility, flexibility, and adaptability in your approach.

Self-doubt is here to protect you and keep you safe...

What if self-doubt is your great protector? What if self-doubt is your soul's voice keeping you safe from something financially, physically, emotionally, or spiritually that you are not prepared to experience or be ready for?

Self-doubt can be that voice that is asking you.

- Are you sure this is ready to go?
- Are you certain you can support this?
- Are you convinced that you have mapped it out?
- Are you positive that you are not cutting corners?
- Is this what you truly want?

Maybe self-doubt is asking you to get some help because you can't do it alone. Instead of falling into the trap that self-doubt is negative, and keeps you stuck, instead get curious. Lean into your self-doubt; you can dance with it, and you can gain strength, courage, and confidence as you tango with your self-doubt. Get familiar with it.

You have a choice. You can allow self-doubt to consume every ounce of you and become your identity .... or you can use self-doubt as a way to catapult you forward.

The greatest obstacle to your success is self-doubt...

Self-doubt can be that deep inquiry that you need to embark on with a level of compassion, understanding and eagerness to comprehend. Turn your mental blocks into building blocks.

Self-doubt has a purpose. It's as simple as asking questions *like "what is the purpose of your self-doubt?" and "how is self-doubt serving you?"*

There are many successful individuals amongst us and very successful people that we look up to, and even aspire to be like who are plagued with self-doubt. Second-guessing themselves, their abilities and their talents are just another step in their daily routine.

While they are too busy doubting themselves, we on the other hand are in *'awe'* of their presence, inspired by how they show up and are intimidated by their full potential. Start today and investigate in what areas of your life are you self-doubting yourself the most.

We all have moments of self-doubt, it's what we do with it...

Once you have identified the area of life that you self-doubt the most. Pay attention, and take note of what you are thinking, feeling and how you are showing up. Get curious, ask thought-provoking questions, and discover the abundant choices that you have before your very eyes.

Then challenge your self-doubt and get to the root cause as to '*why*' it is showing up for you in that area of your life. Plan what actions you need to take in order to change that. It can be as simple as thinking self-doubt is here to keep you safe.

The ability to continue in the presence of self-doubt enhances, strengthens, and boosts your level of resilience and thus recover from any future adversity, difficulties, or any form of hardship. Isn't it time to believe in yourself a little more and go after what you want?

Stop second-guessing yourself...

Always trust your gut. It knows what your head hasn't figured out yet. Overthinking is the biggest cause of our unhappiness. We have all walked that path or experienced it at some stage in our lives. So, what makes us second-guess ourselves?

Well, there is a myriad of reasons as to why. It can be from a lack of trust in oneself, insecurity about one's decision, a lack of confidence or a repeating cycle of self-doubt. I don't know about you, but I have second-guessed myself a good deal of my life. Being the sensitive soul that I am, I have lost count of how many times I have said to myself:

- I wonder if that was the right thing to say
- What about if they misinterpreted what I said and took it out of context?
- What if I had done this instead?
- I wonder if I would have had a different response

And the list goes on. *"What if"* or *"what could have been"* are the norm with most of my weeks. Second-guessing shows up in so many different ways, especially when it comes to making decisions.

A second-guessing mind is known as a false mind…

When we allow thoughts and feelings to flow through with no barriers, no *'buts'* and no restrictions, this is what we call a free-flowing mind. A second-guessing mind is known as a normal human mind, which means that we are getting in the way of our free-flowing mind.

Making a decision can be difficult when there are no alternatives. I get that at times you have to take calculated risks because not taking risks or acting sometimes can mean you lose the opportunity at hand. However, my motto is when you can't make a decision, that is a sure sign to not make one until you feel ready to do so. By putting this into practice, you will find less second-guessing because you have the time to reflect, pause and work through your options.

The way that it works for me is to write a list of pros and cons, so it is out of my head and in front of me. Doubt kills more dreams than failure. Often, I see leaders second-guessing themselves by seeking validation from their external environment, whether they were good enough, smart enough or what others may have thought about them.

You can almost see it in action. Their self-talk or inner dialogue is rambling so loud that it is creating invisible networks that could power a whole city. The inner dialogue sounds a little like this:

- I wonder if they thought I was good enough.
- I wonder if I came across as smart enough like I looked like I knew what I was talking about.
- I wonder if they like me and if I am going to connect with them.
- I wonder if they are going to believe in me and if I will convince them that this is a good idea.

One of the most common ones is, *"I wonder what they are going to think of me?"* When you start seeing your own worth, you will find it harder to stay around people who don't. Consequently, you won't care so much about what others think of you.

Your addiction to validation...

One of my astrology teachers once said, *"seeking external validation is like the sun asking the moon's permission to shine."* She further went on by explaining that we all must stop seeking internal peace, love, and unity through external validation.

Far too often, individuals focus on receiving validation from family, friends, peers, or anyone that they would consider an authority figure. And half the time we don't even realise how often we are doing it. Don't get me wrong, it's okay at times to ask for somebody else's opinions, thoughts, or feelings. It's when we are continuously asking others what they think before making decisions on important matters.

What might happen is that you don't receive the right kind of advice or information, which could have quite an impact on your level of confidence, self-esteem, or motivation. Doing so will have an impact on your own acceptance, belief, and confidence.

Seeking validation will keep you trapped. Imagine you are working on a project. You are asking for so much feedback, validation, and other people's opinions to the point where you are constantly changing the presentation of your project just to please others.

This ends up making your project not look nor feel like your project at all. It has lost your brand, your vision, and your character altogether. Instead, it reflects who the other person is. Which doesn't make them a bad or dismissive person, just unaware. However, imagine this. If you were to go on by your own feelings of what made you feel right and good about what you were doing, you would then be seeking internal validation, uplifting your worth with this inner feeling of knowing that you did an amazing job.

Now, how empowered would you feel right then and there? This is why it is key not to give your power away to others. You need to have your back. You need your own support and infrastructure. Doing so will make you feel stronger, more successful, and more confident. People can think about what they like. Don't desire their validation because it belongs to them after all and as somebody else should save their validation for themselves, you should project your energy toward validating yourself.

Self-doubt builds momentum...

It is dangerously easy to fall into the trap of self-doubt. It all starts with a couple of thoughts about a particular situation. You leave it unaddressed, thinking it is nothing and that it will pass. The self-loathing thoughts then appear regularly enough that you start to forget a time without them. Fuelled with enough emotion, you start to believe that you are inadequate, not good enough, and not smart enough. You are continually searching for reassurance from your external environment.

You may find yourself in a loop of repeating patterns of replaying the past. These are negative incidents that no longer serve you, that carry an unpleasant outcome and make you feel negative about yourself.

So, before going down that rabbit hole, become more conscious of your self-doubts, your second-guessing or your continuous worries about what others think of you. All that does is build the muscle of more uncertainty and an overwhelming sense of hopelessness.

Ultimately, these small actions build up into big problems that prevent you from believing in yourself. Then, this self-doubt builds momentum by creeping into every area of your life, business, and relationships.

Your brain works in two modes—growth and protection. However, it can't be in both. When we are self-doubting or second-guessing ourselves, the brain gets stuck and does not know which road to travel.

Learn to trust yourself…

Make strong decisions. Don't second-guess yourself. If you feel that it is the right thing, then go with your intuition. Your gut is always right. The thing here is to recognise when you are feeling stuck in making a decision. Ask yourself this:

- What is making me puzzled about making the decision?
- What is going on in my mind?
- What am I really feeling?

Our brain thrives on certainty and safety. Consequently, when there is a level of uncertainty, this can become troubling for some people. So, what do we do about it? Knowledge is power. The more awareness one has, the more insight and, therefore, power.

Thus, it is key to gather as much information as possible to move your brain into feeling a little bit safer about you making your decision. The more data and the more facts, the more successful you will be at trusting yourself to move forward with a decision.

Write down the costs and benefits as you collect your data, the consequences and your pros and cons list.

If you find yourself in a situation where it is hard to obtain relevant information, choose to instead rely on what you already know about yourself. Let's imagine you have to conduct a debate on a topic that won't be revealed until presentation day. You may not be able to decide your points yet, however you can rely on the fact that you are quick-witted, a perfect argumentative tool.

Curiosity is key to success…

Experiment and be curious in your approach. Have a wandering mind. Don't get stuck in over-processing, overthinking and overanalysing. The more curious the mind, the further forward thinking. This allows us to be more inquisitive, explorative and test new ways of doing things. Hence why new doors open for us.

Navigate uncertainty with curiosity, deal with what comes up in the present moment and be more conscious of where, when, and how you are second-guessing yourself. A negative element to consider when you second-guess yourself is that it prevents you from fully committing to a decision or action because of fear of failure, which is a result of shame or embarrassment.

One way that I deal with this kind of fear is by bringing it to the surface. I have a good laugh about it to the point where I imagine what could be the most awkward, exasperating, and worrisome situation that could unfold before my very eyes. If I can bring some humour to it and even talk about it, I loosen the boundaries of the fear altogether.

It no longer has power over me.

Rewire your brain for self-compassion...

Compassion is the ultimate expression of your highest self. To do a daily practice of self-compassion through meditation, mindfulness and being present with your thoughts, feelings and experiences is to become an observer of them. In doing so, you must sit there with absolutely no judgement.

Neuroscience tells us that neuroplasticity is the ability to change the structure and function of our brain. In other words, we have the power to rewire our brains and change the way we think and feel.

How does this happen? Well, neurons that fire together, wire together. Once we can be conscious of our thoughts and change them instead of fuelling them with our emotions, we can change our experience.

There have been so many experiments that show how we can change the meaning of a past event in a present moment. We can change the chain reaction from our past and, therefore, change our present and our future.

Second-guessing just creates unnecessary stress, anxiety and has a serious impact on our associations and the meanings we give to life, love, career, and self. Compassion, curiosity, and confidence, on the other hand, enable us to trust our choices and move forward with courage.

The Dalai Lama said it best: *"Compassion is the radicalism of our time."*

Freedom is when you take your mask off...

We all wear a mask depending on what role we are playing at that very instance. We wear our masks for such a long time that we forget who we truly are beneath them. Yet—behind the mask lies the true beauty, you! Have you ever felt like a fraud or a phoney? Have you ever worried that someone would discover that everything you have done is an absolute fluke or a flicker of luck? Have no fear you are not alone.

Most of us have had such an experience whether it is in our career, relationships, or life... the feeling of we are not good enough, not worthy enough or that we don't deserve our success, prosperity, happiness, or accomplishment. It's more common than you think.

You would be surprised that most successful, high-achieving individuals all dance with the Imposter Syndrome regardless of how much they have accomplished, how famous they are or how much success they have obtained. Now that you know it is something that we have all experienced then it's about bringing some light and self-awareness as to when, where and with whom your Imposter Syndrome pops its little head up.

Some of the most common statements are.

- I feel like a lot of my successes were sheer luck!
- I feel like I don't deserve any of the success I have attained
- I feel foolish and very uncomfortable describing my achievements

- I feel like my success doesn't really prove anything
- I feel like I am getting away with something when someone praises me
- I feel like I don't belong around those that have achieved what I aspire to be
- I feel like a fake and worry that others will realise how little I know
- I feel that others deserve more than me

Oscar Wilde says *"man is least himself when he talks in his own person. Give him a mask and he will tell you the truth."*

Behind the mask you live in...

Living authentically begins when you take off the mask that you have been hiding behind. Think about the last time you felt fear and anxiety take control of your day. Maybe it stopped you from speaking up in a meeting because you felt like your opinion wasn't worthwhile or that it may make everyone uncomfortable. Perhaps a simple email took you hours to write because your inner critic kept telling you it didn't sound professional enough—that you weren't good enough.

Believe it or not many high achievers struggle with thoughts and feelings that they are a fraud, incompetent, inadequate, incapable, ineffectual, inefficient, inexperienced and any other *'in'* words that you can think of despite a track record of achievements, accomplishments, and capabilities. Does this all sound too familiar to you? Well, this psychological phenomenon is what is known as Impostor Syndrome, which can show up in many areas of our lives.

Let me ask you this. When you look back on your day or week, what is your point of focus? Do you focus on what went wrong? Or do you focus on, what went well, what are you proud of or what you could have done differently? Imposter Syndrome is the gap between who we see ourselves as being and who we think we need to be, in order to achieve a goal. And... this is where it gets tricky because confidence is about what we can and can't do whereas the Imposter Syndrome is about who we think we are. They are perfect dancing partners.

To truly set yourself free from Imposter Syndrome, you need to identify your blocks to be able to break through each one and thus allow yourself to shift your perception of yourself. This will allow you to see you are already that person that you think you are not, ultimately closing the gap and freeing yourself to show up as all of who you really are.

Dr Valerie Young found there are 5 different personality types of Imposter Syndrome, all of which will be explored in the section below.

Strive for progress not perfection...

In this chapter, we have covered quite a bit of content when it comes to perfectionism.

The first type of Imposter Syndrome is *'The Perfectionists'*. These are the individuals who aim for perfection and who often experience high levels of anxiety, doubt, and worry when they fail to achieve their extreme goals. Perfectionists are usually dissatisfied with their work because they tend to focus on areas where they could have done better, rather than celebrate the things they did well. That is due to setting extremely high expectations for themselves, and even if they meet 99% of their goals, more often than not they will still feel like failures. Regardless of the magnitude of the mistake, it usually ends with them always questioning their own competence and worth as a person.

The next personality types are *'The Expert'*. Upon finishing a task, the expert will not feel satisfied until they know everything there is to know about the subject. Experts continuously hunt for new information, which prevents them from completing tasks and projects. Those who avoid applying for a job because they do not meet every requirement may fall into the expert category. Experts feel the need to know every piece of information before they start a project and constantly look for new certifications or training to improve their skills. They won't apply for a job if they don't meet all the criteria in the posting, and they might be hesitant to ask a question in class or speak up in a meeting at work because they're afraid of looking stupid if they don't already know the answer.

The hidden habits of natural genius...

The next personality type is *'The Natural Genius'* ... Natural geniuses are typically able to master a new skill quickly and easily, and they often feel ashamed, talentless, and weak when they cannot. People who fall into this category fail to recognise that nearly everyone needs to build upon their skills throughout life to succeed. When the *'natural geniuses'* have to struggle or work hard to accomplish something, they think this means they aren't good enough or that this particular activity or achievement is not meant for them. They are used to skills coming easily, and when they have to put in the effort, their brain tells them that's proof they're an impostor.

The fourth personality type is *'The Soloist'* ... The soloist may also be known as the rugged individualist. They prefer to work alone and tend to believe that asking for help will reveal their incompetence. A soloist will typically turn down help so that they can prove their worth as an individual. Soloists feel they have to accomplish tasks on their own, and if they need to ask for help, they think that means they are a failure or a fraud. A soloist when offered help will always say *"no"* because they see this as a sign of weakness.

There is a superhero in all of us...

The final personality types are *'The Superhero'* ... Superheroes often excel in all areas, mainly because they push themselves so hard. Many workaholics can be classed as superheroes. This overload of work will eventually result in burnout, which can affect physical health, mental well-being, and relationships with others. Superheroes push themselves to work harder than those around them to prove that they're not impostors.

They feel the need to succeed in all aspects of life—at work, as parents, as partners—and may feel stressed when they are not accomplishing something.

I am sure that you can by now see the importance of why you need to understand Imposter Syndrome and its attributes. According to Hal Stone, PhD and Sidra Stone, PhD research, these are the top twelve traits of the inner critic:

1. It constricts your ability to be creative.
2. It stops you from taking risks because it makes you fear failure.
3. It views your life as a series of mistakes waiting to happen.
4. It undermines your courage to change.
5. It compares you unfavourably with others and makes you feel 'less than'.
6. It is terrified of being shamed and so monitors all your behaviour to avoid this.
7. It causes you to suffer from low self-esteem, and possibly depression because it tells you that you are not good enough.
8. It can make looking at yourself in a mirror or shopping for clothes miserable because of its ability to create such a negative view of the body.
9. It can take all the fun out of life with its criticisms.
10. It makes self-improvement a compulsive chore because it bases the work on the premise that something is wrong with you.
11. It doesn't allow you to take in the good feelings that other people have towards you.
12. It makes you susceptible, and often a victim, to the judgments of other people.

Banish your inner critic...

Your inner critic is simply a part of you that needs more love. Jay Early, PhD and Bonnie Weiss found that there are seven types of inner critics.

Perfectionist

- This critic tries to get you to do things perfectly.
- It sets high standards for the things you produce and has difficulty saying something is complete and letting it go out to represent your best work.
- It tries to make sure that you fit in and that you will not be judged or rejected.
- Its expectations probably reflect those of people who have been important to you in the past.

Inner Controller

- This critic tries to control your impulses: eating, drinking, sexual activity, etc.
- It is polarised with an indulger—an addict who it fears can get out of control at any moment.
- It tends to be harsh and shaming in an effort to protect you from yourself.
- It is motivated to try to make you a good person who is accepted and functions well in society.

Taskmaster

- This critic wants you to work hard and be successful.
- It fears that you may be mediocre or lazy and will be judged a failure if it does not push you to keep going.
- Its pushing often activates a procrastinator or a rebel that fights against its harsh dictates.

Underminer

- This critic tries to undermine your self-confidence and self-esteem so that you won't take risks.

- It makes direct attacks on your self-worth so that you will stay small and not take chances where you could be hurt or rejected.
- It is afraid of your being too big or too visible and not being able to tolerate judgement or failure.

Destroyer

- It makes pervasive attacks on your fundamental self-worth.
- It shames you and makes you feel inherently flawed and not entitled to basic understanding or respect.
- This most debilitating criticism comes from early life deprivation or trauma.
- It is motivated by a belief that it is safer not to exist.

Guilt-Tripper

- This critic is stuck in the past. It is unable to forgive you for wrongs you have done or people you have hurt.
- It is concerned about relationships and holds you to standards of behaviour prescribed by your community, culture, and family.
- It tries to protect you from repeating past mistakes by making sure you never forget or feel free.

Conformist

- This critic tries to get you to fit into a certain mould based on standards held by society, your culture, or your family.
- It wants you to be liked and admired and to protect you from being abandoned, shamed, or rejected.
- The conformist fears that the rebel or the free spirit in you would act in ways that are unacceptable. So, it keeps you from being in touch with and expressing your true nature.

Which inner critic can you relate to? And why? Did you know that self-sabotaging thoughts and behaviours are created by your inner critic? Therefore, the more conscious and aware of your thoughts, the more you can control your inner critic.

Don't stand in your own way...

Self-sabotage is when we say we want something and then we make sure that it doesn't happen for some reason. This can come in the form of procrastination when you leave everything to the very last minute for instance. Then, if you don't do well on the test or the project, you can say, "*Well what can you expect? I only started on it last night. If I had more time I would have done better.*" "*I clearly didn't try at all.*"

Another form of self-sabotage is over-committing. Saying "*yes*" to everything, being busy for the sake of being busy. Life, in general, is moving way too fast. How often have you caught yourself saying, "*oh, my golly gosh, I can't believe it's February already!*" Or you meet up with a friend whom you haven't seen for ages only to catch yourself saying, "*My, hasn't Katelyn gotten so big! What are you feeding her?*" Life just got too busy.

We are accelerating at an alarming speed. When we live at full throttle, we disrupt our own natural rhythms in a way that prevents us from listening to our inner calling. Our body posture is unconsciously tight. We get smaller and smaller, to the point where we don't appreciate the beauty around us and all the experiences and gifts in our lives. Instead, we are continuously seeking externally and asking ourselves, "*what's next?*"

Busy is the new stupid. There is this standard that we constantly need to be doing something or we need to be on our way somewhere else. We feel important if we are busy. At times, we feel that we are judged based on how busy we are, not so much on how productive or effective we are. After all, we achieve one task, tick, done! Then we seek the next big endeavour. '*What is my next priority?*'

We are on this hamster wheel striving for fulfilment and looking in all the wrong places. Let me break it to you gently. You are not a hamster, so get off the wheel and slow down to live the life you were born to live.

You must be perfect, mistakes are bad...

Where does it all come from? Early in your life the significant people around you, your parents, siblings, and teachers play a huge role in forming your expectations, beliefs, and self-image. You learn what is valued, what gets approval and, very importantly, what gets disapproval. Your imposter feelings and the Imposter Syndrome probably have their origins in your early life experiences.

If you were rewarded for being perfect and missed out if less than perfect, then you will find mistakes are very scary. They prove that you are not perfect, which might mean losing the approval of significant people.

Being overpraised – If you are feted for everything you do, told how clever you are, and how you will achieve great things, then you can get a bit worried about what will happen if you don't live up to these great expectations. Will people still like you if you don't achieve? People in this situation may also feel as though they cannot be successful without a helping hand or in other terms, being coddled or overly praised.

Low expectations – If you have been told that you are not bright, not athletic, or not good at maths, your expectations have been lowered. Then when you do end up in university, or in an important role, you can feel that you don't belong. People like us don't go to university or get important jobs.

Fear of failure – You worry that if you try something and it doesn't work, the shame and humiliation will be unbearable. The courage to get back up and try again will be almost nil.

Fear of success – You worry that if you try something and it does work, things will change. Perhaps people won't like you anymore because you have allowed success to consume you and make you boastful. Perhaps the expectations and pressure will increase.

For imposters, making mistakes is bad, extremely bad. It is the time when you risk being exposed. So somewhere along the line, you picked up the belief that mistakes are not okay. And since mistakes are a part of life, you have a problem. And so, you feel like an imposter.

It's time to detox your ego...

Do things that feed your soul, not your ego, and you will be happy. We all have egos, right? But do you know what your ego is sabotaging? It could be sabotaging your relationships, or that promotion you always wanted. Having a big ego can be hard to admit, because most of us associate having a BIG ego with being, well, rude. But the thing is we all have an ego—but when we balance ego with soul, we find a happier, less competitive, more peaceful, more loving way of life.

How big is your ego? Time for an honesty check... Let's see if you have a BIG ego.

- Do you put people down (*directly and in your head*) in order to feel powerful?
- Do you think you are better than everyone else?
- Do you use your positional power to get things done?
- And are you always critical of others' work or achievements?

If you answered *"yes"* to all those questions, then the answer is *"yes"* you have a super BIG ego. But, because YOU are the solution to all your problems because you put them there in the first place. YOU can do something about this.

The ego is usually a mask for a lack of self-love. It's a kind of defensive mechanism. When we start to accept ourselves as the glorious messes, startling geniuses, loving creators and *'works in progress'* that we all are, and I mean truly accept ourselves, we can start to let go of the *'ego'*.

Loving yourself isn't vanity, it is sanity...

Self-love is a fickle thing—it can come and go, but if you work on it, and even embrace those times when you stuff up, you can master self-love. Be your best friend, your confidant, spend time with yourself—learn to understand what makes you *'tick'* and understand that you are beautiful, uniquely you. A powerful human being equipped for life and everything it throws at you!

When you begin to like yourself, you can start to love yourself, and believe in yourself. When I refer to believing in yourself, I don't mean citing it with empty feelings. Genuinely feel it and know deep within and without a doubt that you can do anything.

In all honesty, if I was to ask you to rate yourself out of ten, how much do you love yourself, what would it be? And why? Self-love is not selfish. Self-love is knowing yourself and liking yourself anyway, and the really important thing about that is all of those fulfilling relationships that you want—with your mother, your sister, your partner, your children ... they will continue to elude you until you can love yourself.

To fall in love with yourself is the first best-kept secret to happiness... and yet most of us still keep searching for love elsewhere—external to ourselves, in the form of approval, compliments, achievements and recognition, and all this does is feed the ego. It does nothing to fulfil our soul.

Self-love is the greatest medicine...

And here's why. Because your ego holds you back from the things you really want to say, the things that your heart is bursting at the seams to sing, like, *"I love you" "I miss you"* or *"I am sorry."* Ego gets in the way of you putting your emotions on display. Because you're scared of rejection or disappointment. But when you truly love yourself and feel content with who you are, you know, instinctively, that to love ... doesn't need love in return, and you are perfectly wonderful the way you are, with or without the acceptance of others.

It's hard to understand this until you actually begin to live it. But once you do, you'll find joy and delight in places you didn't know existed. You'll be bursting with confidence and self-assuredness that is soul-fed and not driven by ego. Life will become less about how you look and more about how you feel.

How to diminish the ego? If you find it a little hard to connect with self-love, there are things you can do to help diminish the ego. The first is to be *'humble'* – which reminds me of a quote a teacher once taught me – *"the meek shall rule the earth."*

It takes little steps .... for example, instead of thinking of yourself all the time, why not be of service to others, completely let go of your needs and wants - instead, be a beacon of light for others. Randomly go and volunteer for a cause that you only just found out existed. Don't even think, just do it. Another really cool way to detox your ego is to go into everything with a *'learning'* mindset. Go into all interactions with the assumption that you are going to learn something, which is very different from thinking that you know it all .... You'll also benefit from opening up the learning receptors of your precious brain.

Or ... how about, *'seek to understand'*. You can only do this by listening with your ears, eyes, and heart. Ask more questions, so you can learn from others ... not only will you undoubtedly learn something new, but it will also make others feel valued, heard, and understood in return.

Appreciation and encouragement go a long way toward loving thy self. But people can also discern the difference between *'authenticity'* and not. When you're genuinely open to another person, they can feel the energy as positive and receptive. They know when a connection is being made and whether the interaction is something you want to be renewed.

Keep your ego on a short leash and live from your soul…

The ego finds what it wants in words and the soul finds what it needs in silence… It's very healthy to be *'aware'* of your ego and to check in with whether it is you or your ego acting out to certain scenarios that no longer serve you.

Let's investigate the difference between the two. The soul seeks to serve others and the ego seeks to serve itself and seeks for external recognition. The soul sees life in general as a *'gift'* and the ego sees everything as a competition and will do whatever it takes to win! The soul, on the other hand, enjoys the *'learnings'* along its merry way, during its journey.

As a leader, partner, or parent, check in with what is driving you. Do the things that feed your soul and not your ego, and you will be happier, more influential, and more abundant because you as the soul focus on the *'we'* – whereas the ego focuses on the *'me'*.

Your ego is not your amigo... put simply, your ego is not your friend. Why? Because it's not grounded in love and compassion. It needs to win all the time and be right all of the time. If the ego doesn't get its way, it is often offended and therefore becomes quite *'judgemental'* about everything, and sometimes vengeful. But .... If we apply the concept of *'perception is projection'*, you can begin to understand that if you have a tendency to be highly critical of others, you, yourself, have a very strong inner critic. As a result, you project the critic external of yourself to feel superior.

The ego is powerful .... the more airtime you give it, the bigger it becomes. The ego is never satisfied, it never rests, it always wants more and is constantly comparing with others and always identifying success by their achievements.

A healthy, balanced ego understands when it is not doing well—a healthy ego takes feedback and is very self-aware because it knows when it is beginning to judge ... by acknowledging that when one finger is pointing at another person... there are three fingers pointing right back at you!

Eckhart Tolle said, *"that ego is no longer ego when you know there is ego."*

A little more kindness and a little less judgement…

We all have an ego, so we need to integrate and work with it. Balance is the key to developing a healthy ego. We can't get rid of it; we are bound together for life. But a healthy ego allows us to grow up with a loving sense of self. It accepts the dichotomy that resides in every single one of us, helping us solve problems creatively. It gives us the capacity to develop meaningful relationships because we understand that an unhealthy ego is like a shield, protecting us from the outside world, but also preventing us from loving ourselves, our lives, and others.

An unhealthy ego will tell you to stick to what's comfortable. It likes to avoid uncertainty and has unrealistic expectations of yourself and others. An unhealthy ego is rooted in fear, anxiety, limiting beliefs, and toxic thinking patterns.

And this is why you need to starve your ego and feed your soul. Together they make strange bedfellows – they are not always comfortable together, but you can work with each to create harmony, knowing when your ego is present and what you need it for, and feeding your soul, so it steps up, and keeps your ego in check!

Do not confuse the voice of ego with that of intuition…

An unhealthy ego never feels good enough. It uses anger to communicate, so it's very reactive and defensive because it is driven by fear instead of love. It tends to blame everyone and avoids those courageous conversations. It is highly critical and avoids apologising. The ego has a chip on its shoulder, it feels a sense of entitlement or grandiosity, and is unable to demonstrate compassion or understanding towards people who hold different opinions or beliefs. An unhealthy ego knows how to wear a mask!

A healthy ego is resilient, happy, and thinks before it speaks, it has time to ponder, reflect and think in terms of possibilities. A healthy ego is optimistic in nature, sees that everything (*even failure*) is an opportunity, seeks to understand, appreciate and comes across as strong, curious, and confident ... it knows it can handle any tricky situation. It knows how to embrace imperfections and practices acceptance, compassion, and cooperation, with integrity and authenticity!

When our ego is healthy, we can navigate challenging moments in life, sit in vulnerability and not be overcome by fear. A healthy ego allows us to genuinely appreciate our strengths, accept our imperfections, and love ourselves unconditionally. Developing enough ego to believe in ourselves—the key here is whenever we observe ourselves reacting to any event, trigger, person, or environment, we must learn to stop, pause and ask ourselves, *"Why am I reacting this way?"*

This is the only way for us to backtrack from our emotions and thoughts to our memories, which hold our influence, root cause and provenance of emotional programming. The results will be unearthing emotions that we may have been repressing for years, such as anger, sadness, fear, guilt, shame, and grief.

Only when we connect with these repressed emotions can we commence the healing process. But how can we heal? By identifying and integrating the wounded parts of ourselves. For example:

- Fear calls for us to be more courageous
- Suffering invites us to be more resilient
- Anger is a calling for us to be more passionate
- Guilt can open the way for being more forgiving
- Shame can point us in the direction of self-love
- Grief can pave the way to acceptance
- Sadness is an opportunity to bring more happiness into our lives and really get into the heart of what makes us happy

Your ego is like a mirror...

Clearly, connecting with our ego is necessary. However, we must understand that our ego does not like to be observed. Consequently, there will be an initial level of resistance. But it is the only way to make the ego consciousness. With this in mind, what we are about to practise is the detachment of the ego. We want to be able to work with it and even dance with it.

First, you have to name your ego as a way of separating yourself from it. This can be as easy as asking your ego, *"what is your name?"* and listening to the first word that comes to mind. Once you have your name, it's time to work with your ego by asking it some very simple questions. The way I like to do that is through journaling.

My first question to my ego would be, *"what are some of your triggers?"* Then, I would write them all down in my journal. If you have lots of words, put them in groups so they have a theme or a headline for you to work with. Now, here comes the fun part. Besides every answer, write down the emotions that the ego experienced with each trigger.

Finally, ask the ego, *"what was the meaning you gave to each event?"* and write the answers next to each one. For example, my trigger was my husband taking over my cooking, the emotion I experienced was an annoyance and the meaning I gave it was that I am not competent in cooking and not worthy of consideration.

Throughout this entire process, we are observing and work with our ego to give it a different meaning.

The person is not their behaviour...

Ultimately, your ego is here to protect you. Once we can appreciate and accept that our ego wants the best for us, it is easier to put ourselves in its shoes. From there, we can identify what needs are not being met and why our ego is showing up in a certain way.

Doing so, also helps us become more forgiving and less judgemental with others. For example, if we go back to my dearest husband, he was just trying to help me. The story that came with it was my baggage, not him. As Carl Jung said, *"we marry our own unconscious mind and then we project all of our unresolved baggage onto our partners."* It is so much more empowering when we realise this and can own up to it.

In the words of Debbie Ford, when you understand projection, you will never see the world the same way again. In this holographic world, everyone and everything is a mirror, and you are always seeing yourself and talking to yourself. If you choose, you can now look at what emotionally affects you as an alarm, a clue to uncover your shadow, a catalyst for growth that gives you an opportunity to reclaim a hidden aspect of yourself.

In closing of this chapter, I will leave you with a powerful quote for reflection: Do not judge my story by the chapter you walked in on.

Chapter 5
Activating Your Intuitive Intelligence...

"One does not become enlightened by imagining figures of light, but by making the darkness conscious" – **Carl Jung**

Whether you call it a gut feeling, a sixth sense, a hunch, an instinct, or an inner knowing—intuitive intelligence is real. We all experience it often. However, most of us are either not aware of it or we fight with it by allowing our minds to get in our way.

Know this my dearest ones: our intuitive intelligence is playing out every single day—it's how we make decisions. It guides us on whether to go left or right, what school to choose or a new restaurant to pick. Our intuition will always be our highest form of intelligence.

Most of us can activate our intuitive intelligence just by being conscious of its very existence. The more we use it, the more it becomes our superpower. If we choose to ignore it, we simply lose its benefits and guiding tools, leaving many decisions up to us instead.

So, how do you even know if your intuitive intelligence is working with you and not against you? It can be as simple as picking up what others are putting down, without uttering a word. You may be one of those intuitive people that can walk into a room and sense the emotions bottled up around you. The saying *"you can cut the air with a knife!"* when referring to a tense atmosphere is a perfect example of intuition. It means you can automatically sense other feelings without necessarily needing clear physical or emotional cues.

The flip side to you picking up on other people's feelings is that you end up carrying their emotional baggage. Have you ever been around other individuals after investing a good amount of time with them and then walk away feeling depleted or elevated? This is you picking up on what they are putting down. You know those individuals that lift you up after investing a few hours with them—you walk out skipping to your car. Well, the opposite of that can also happen when you are around individuals that suck the life out of you, these are known as energy vampires. They sure do exist!

You may have crossed paths with an energy vampire...

Well, if you have felt completely drained, depleted, or exhausted around a particular person, for no apparent reason then guess what? You my dearest have crossed paths with an energy vampire. Now no need to stock up on garlic or visit your local church for some holy water, a stake or a golden cross, we aren't talking about those kinds of vampires. The ones that we speak about are the *'energy'* vampires.

There is no need to panic or fear such a phenomenon. Research shows that energy vampires are only attracted to you because they unconsciously desire to resolve a deeper problem within their psyche, perceiving you as the solution to their problems. The best thing you can do is to have a little compassion, understanding and strong boundaries.

Energy vampires receive an increased amount of energy around other people, and therefore at times, you feel exhausted, tired, or exasperated for no identifiable reason. These energy vampires, whether consciously or unconsciously, evoke emotions in others just to feed on the triggered emotional energy.

Yep! It sounds calculated and malice, but these people exist. They are not considerate because all they think is about themselves, lacking empathy, compassion, warmth, understanding, consideration, and more evidential emotional maturity.

Compassion is to look beyond your own pain...

By the way, *'compassion'* is not a sign of weakness. Quite the contrary, it is a sign of strength and can be very useful if we can look beyond our own pain, needs, and wants.

Having empathy by putting yourself in the shoes of another, including the energy vampire, we can understand that their wrongdoings are just a projection of their own pain and insecurities. Therefore, whether consciously or unconsciously, they are addicted to preying on the vitality of others in an attempt to heal their own inner suffering.

If you are a highly empathetic, caring individual like me, you should know that is a sure invitation to attract energy vampires into your life. Empaths often have a hard time setting boundaries due to not wanting to upset the apple cart, thus making them an easy target for energy vampires wherever they lead.

By the way, I am not trying to install fear into your being that is not my intention but more to make you consciously aware that these individuals do exist, and some are masters at it. Some are obsessive and will stop at nothing to steal your energy while they are given access to it.

Compassion isn't about solutions...

Another interesting fact is that when you feel compassion towards someone who might deserve otherwise, they too drop their guard and become compassionate towards you. When you do this, you are flexing your *'compassion'* muscle. Instead of being upset, angry or annoyed with someone because of their behaviour towards you, you could instead transform that energy and immediately witness a difference.

When you sit generating resentment and accusation ... then guess what? That person or situation will continue to annoy you! Compassion is a trained response. Most of the time we automatically feel wronged or hurt in negative situations. This is simply human. But if you keep in mind that compassion can change EVERYTHING, you'll want to use it more. And, when you use it more, the better you'll become at it. Compassion is the key to making YOU happy, and others around you HAPPY.

Energy vampires' prey on others because they are in pain...

Compassion can also help raise and keep your vibrational frequency high. Although you may be tempted with lower vibrational frequencies such as bitterness, belligerent and resentment towards energy vampires, it's important to remember that they haven't developed the capacity to deal with their own demons yet! It is an unconscious act of survival.

The most important thing that you must do is always keep your vibrational frequencies as high as possible – frequencies of peace, joy, love, acceptance and all those feel-good high vibes!

This a message for empaths and an important one of that – it's not your responsibility to solve other people's issues, they are responsible for sorting out their own struggles. Otherwise, you are robbing them of their own lesson, and learnings, getting in the way of them finding their own solution. Trying to solve other people's problems isn't just a bad habit—it's a deeply-rooted need tied up in our own emotions and unconscious biases.

You will most definitely know when you are around energy vampires. They leave you feeling drained, depleted in some way, weary in your thinking, a little anxious and at times irritable.

This is where having strong boundaries are of great importance. There comes a time when you must draw the line somewhere and know when *'enough is enough'*.

The best way to do that is to understand the different types of energy vampires that exist. Carl Jung understood the Universal archetypes as the ancient language, patterns and representations derived from the collective unconscious and that every relationship brings forth psychological and emotional energy vampires. These types of energy vampires feed off the life force of others... it may sound all doom and gloom, but I promise this information will change your life if applied. There are many more that I talk about in the shadow workshop (*more information in chapter 7*) however, I think the six below will give you a good starting point.

Victim energy vampires' prey off your guilt...

This kind of energy vampire doesn't know the meaning of accountability, rather they like to blame, shame, and put the responsibilities on someone else's shoulders. They are the manipulators of the energy vampires; they do not understand the concept of boundaries and they are relentless in their pursuit of what they want—and they have no regard for who gets hurt along the way.

But it doesn't stop there. They resort to emotional blackmail to get their own way because they know that using fear, obligation and guilt is the best way to control another person. The internal driver of this socially impaired behaviour is a lack of self-esteem.

These individuals are constantly second-guessing themselves; they have a low level of self-confidence and when we peel back the layers, they feel unworthy, unaccepted, and unloved thus seeking all of the *'un'* words external to themselves. Because they were not shown sufficient love, validation, and approval as children, they go out of their way to make others feel sorry for them.

Always keep an eye out for their self-pity cues and don't get involved, instead reduce your time with these individuals and do not entertain such conversations.

Narcissist energy vampires' have no capacity to show empathy...

A narcissist energy vampire never likes to be beaten, bettered, or defeated; they are not too keen on sharing the spotlight. It's all about them! Narcissist energy vampires always struggle with the fact that the world must revolve around them—and they will always be accusing someone else of ruining their life. It is invariably the same person the narcissist energy vampire is trying to destroy.

They find it difficult to feel genuine happiness for another human being —as a result, they draw energy from other individuals to nourish, provide and satisfy their own emotional needs. In other words, they suck the goodness out of you—if you let them.

Narcissist energy vampires are experts in manipulation—and they know how to turn on the charm—they say the right things, they do the right things, they behave friendly and sincere in order to obtain something that they want or need and in doing so are deceiving you.

They expect you to feed their ego—conversations are all about them. I am sure we have all had those experiences where an individual is so self-absorbed that you think surely there must be more than this as a conversation. If you ever feel disempowered around individuals in any way, shape or form, the best bet is not to feed their ego, limit contact with them and if possible, cut your ties with them completely.

Dominator energy vampires' love to be in control...

Then there are the control freaks who love to dominate, govern, or rule and in doing so, intimidate those around them. These dominator energy vampires are known for their airs of superiority. They think they are better than everyone else!

They come across as boastful, confident—a big personality if you will, when really, they are feeling very insecure with themselves and experience jealousy in relationships, feel doubtful and hold onto grudges from being hurt or wronged in the past. Thus, this vampire harbours anger, resentment, and bitterness which in turn projects those emotions onto others by taking control of others.

Due to their deep insecurities, they have rigid beliefs, ideologies and a fixed mindset which makes them very cynical, discriminatory, and prejudiced about life in general. If you are around these kinds of energy vampires ... the obvious answer would be to limit contact with the individual and always be on your guard. Remember they will do whatever it takes to put you down so that they feel better about themselves. But keep in mind they are deeply hurting and projecting their pain onto you.

Whoever demoralises, humiliates, or dishonours others is actually doing that to themselves. Not that we should accommodate such behaviour but understand that they are twice as hard on themselves and if they don't want to help themselves—self-pity is a dead-end road.

Melodramatic energy vampires thrive on drama...

These energy vampires go out of their way to create problems because they love drama! Yep! Day and night because they need to fulfil the emptiness, abandoned and deprived void that they feel inside.

Any form of catastrophe, confrontation or crisis turns them on, they love problematic situations because it gives them a reason to feel victimised as they are in deep need of love. They crave to be in the spotlight and go about it in a very theatrical dramatic way to achieve such attention.

These are the individuals that drain your energy by sucking you into their drama—they are literally addicted to drama like the brain is addicted to sugar. Those lower vibrational emotional frequencies such as anger, jealousy, resentment, loneliness, and annoyance are regularly featured in their intense lives.

The best way to deal with these individuals is to not take sides, decline and withdraw from getting involved with any drama, create distance, and once again remove them from your life if possible. And... if you feel yourself getting pulled into their drama, check in with yourself. What's the trigger that is drawing you into their drama? There's some shadow work right there for you to integrate.

Judgemental energy vampires love to criticise and pick on others...

Remember everything we judge in others is something within ourselves that we don't want to face. These judgemental energy vampires love to lash out at people, criticise them, belittle them and make others feel small—and this is all due to their extremely low sense of self-worth and low self-esteem.

How they treat others is clearly a projection of how they treat and feel about themselves—or they themselves are the victim of bullying. These judgemental energy vampires are predators as they prey, chase and pillage others—they are the bullies of the energy vampires.

Often these energy vampires are insecure about themselves and find temporary relief and satisfaction when judging others—it makes them feel superior. Judging others is a boost to their ego!

Never take these judgemental energy vampires to heart, meaning anything they have to say about you, any criticism or disapproval is not to be taken personally. Keep in mind when you get defensive with any of their projections, you are giving your power away. Which means they have won the battle and you lose. However, keeping your cool will throw them off balance.

Innocent energy vampires are overly dependent on others...

Not all energy vampires are vengeful or nasty, there are innocent energy vampires that have no idea that they are taking from you. Those friends that depend and rely on you just a little too much! It's great to be wanted, or even needed, as a matter of fact, however, if you truly cared for these innocent energy vampires, you would encourage them to *'walk a mile'* in their own shoes. You must encourage them to become self-reliant, self-sufficient, and self-supporting.

Because if you are at their beck and call, day, and night... solving all of their problems and being their *'rock'* sort of speaking, eventually it will wear you down and deteriorate your evenly efficient energy source. As a result, you will have no energy to support your own needs.

Although these energy vampires are not aware of what they do, it is of great importance to guide them to work with their own internal guidance. They can bounce ideas off you once they have come to their own understanding and solutions to any problems. You don't have to be a full-time guide, that would be exhausting, time-consuming and not leave enough time for you.

Your sixth sense should be your first sense...

Now that we have covered all the energy vampires, you can see how utilising your intuitive intelligence will assist you to get out of any sticky situation. Intuition is the highest form of intelligence and by activating your intuition by simply feeling your way through life—you are less likely to bump up against any awkward situations. And... by using your intuitive intelligence you will pick up on things ahead of time. These energy vampires truly exist, they are regarded as psychological archetypes.

We are all intuitive beings; some of us are clairvoyant *'clear seeing'* where we will see our archetypes as images, while we are daydreaming; then there are some that are clairaudient *'clear hearing'* where they will hear the soft whispers of their archetypes.

Others may be clairsentient *'clear feeling'* where they will feel their archetypes tapping them gently on the shoulder guiding them. Then there are some that are claircognizance *'clear knowing'* where they may ask a question and out of the blue the answer just drops in. Most of the time this happens when they are busy being creative but there is an inner knowing that their archetypes are giving them signs.

We just have to be *'present'* enough to be able to identify these deeply unconscious archetypal energies and explore them by seeing how they affect our behaviour. We do this by being mindful of our thoughts, feelings, attitudes and therefore being conscious of how we are showing up. The signs are there, we just have to tap into them.

There are no such things as coincidences...

Serendipity, coincidence, and synchronicities are signs that you are on your path. A key component of being intuitive is self-awareness, meaning those that are more self-aware tend to be more intuitive. For those that are not aware of their intuition, have no fear because intuition will never abandon you, desert or leave you... it will go out of its way to capture your attention by externalising itself, showing up as signs from the Universe that leave you in amazement and wonder.

Intuition will always make itself known internally first. If you are not paying attention or are totally ignoring those little nudges, then it will make sure to get your attention by tripping you over with external things to give you a little shake. But... and a big but... if you commit to strengthening your intuition, it will only get stronger.

This is why it is of great importance to pay attention to the signs in your life. When we are not resisting life and we allow life to unfold before our very eyes, there is an expanded commonness, recurrence, and prevalence of synchronicities .... Which basically tells us we are on track, on our path .... well and truly on our journey.

Where there is power, there is resistance...

When we resist, combat, or refuse change .... We remain stuck in our old ways, our old patterns and old programs which create fewer synchronicities ... they don't appear as often. But what about if we embraced the uncertainty, the unpredictable and the unexpected? Now that is the path to true freedom.

Quite often I hear individuals say, *"how come I never experience synchronicities?"* Well, my dearest, the very reason is that you are resisting life, you are denying what you deserve—and you are opposing change due to a fear of failure or even fear of success, afraid of being your authentic self.

The Law of Attraction states that *'like attracts like'* ... meaning whatever you resist will persist. Attempting to push certain experiences away only serves to draw more of the same experiences to you. By focusing on what we don't want, we attract more of its kind. It does sound very counterproductive but it's true, let's bring it to life with an example.

You find yourself paying off debts, constantly rotating on a hamster wheel with a yo-yo budget. All you focus on is all the things that you don't have, whether it's a lack of money, resources or even help. This is what is called a scarcity mindset. The more you try running away from this mindset, the more you will keep attracting it. But if we want to flip this paradigm on its head, then all we have to do is shift to an abundance mindset. View life as a place of growth and opportunity, practise gratitude on a daily basis and then see the positive outcomes from such practice.

Synchronistic meetings are like mirrors that reflect something of ourselves. If we want to grow spiritually, all we have to do is take a good look at ourselves. *"Synchronicity holds the promise that if we want to change inside, the patterns of our external life will change as well"* – Jean Shinoda Bolen

Intuition is the whisper of your soul…

Intuition is a process that gives us the ability to know something instinctively without any analytical thinking or reasoning—it's the bridge between the conscious and unconscious parts of our mind….

And the weird thing here is that most of us are too afraid to say, *"Hey… I don't feel right about this person or this business opportunity"* because we have no hard evidence. Nothing, zilch, nada… except for that strong gut feeling that is intangible. Even though it has been proven time after time that our intuition is often a better decision-maker than our rational mind.

When we do find the courage to speak up about our feelings, we often find ourselves unable to put our finger on exactly why something or someone feels bad. All we are left with is that strong gut feeling.

Carl Jung tells us that our intuition is one of the most powerful mechanisms of our brain. He explains that to be at our optimal functioning state of living, we must *'trust'* our intuition over our rational mind and be able to express our gut feeling. We've all been there, where intuitively you know within your heart of hearts that little voice was telling you to stay clear away from an individual or say *"no"* to a project for a good, unknown reason. And regardless of the cues, you ignored your intuition only to find yourself, in the end, saying to yourself *"I told you so!"*

Intuition is the only true guide in life...

There is a significant amount of research that our gut is connected to the deepest part of our mind—our unconscious mind. It is here to keep us *'safe'* and it remembers EVERYTHING! And, it is connected to a higher mind, higher consciousness and it is connected to our repeating patterns. Therefore, it makes sense to listen to our *'intuition'*, especially when it is the guiding light that keeps us mentally, emotionally, and physically safe.

In fact, way back in time, before book learning, research projects, Gantt charts, spreadsheets, and pie charts, humans were much more adept at using this internal resource—they relied more upon it for decision-making than any other kind of *'proof'*.

But in our modern lives, we're used to gathering data—which is all well and good (*for example, if you want a new pair of $300 shoes and your rent is due, perhaps it would be better not to purchase them*) but intuition plays a strong role in personal decisions.

You know the truth by the way it feels...

Give yourself permission to be led by your intuition—tap into your feelings and tune into that soft little whisper before making any big decisions.

Allow your intuition to guide you, to walk across that *'bridge'* to your unconscious mind that holds your entire bank of memories and experiences. Because you are uniquely you, this will enable you to make the safest decision.

Tuning into your intuition is incredibly important for developing intelligence and making robust, important decisions. *"Synchronicity is an ever-present reality for those who have eyes to see"* – Carl Jung.

Summarised as meaningful coincidences by Jung – at its most awesome, synchronicity can clarify decisions, leading to choices that feel aligned with the best version of yourself.

So how do you do this?

Simply listen to your thoughts and feelings when making important decisions. Your intuition isn't loud but is rather a distinct whisper. And therefore, the practice of mindfulness or meditation, coupled with journaling, is key to tapping into that greatest part of yourself.

When you do the deep work, don't be surprised if your ego or inner critic jumps in. This voice is a little bit louder because it's used to us listening to it. Listening to your intuition takes a little more practice, time, and patience—it exists in all of us, it is simply waiting for us to pay attention!

When you allow your intuition to guide you every day in life, you will create a new, stronger, and deeper relationship with yourself. It will also help you clarify that inner voice and allow you to bring your true intuitive awareness back into your rational everyday life.

Albert Einstein said – *"The only real valuable thing is intuition. The intuitive mind is a sacred gift… and the rational mind is a faithful servant. We have created a society that honours the servant and has forgotten the gift."*

Clear signs that your manifestations are on their way…

A very dear friend of mine once shared that intuition is your inner compass—your guidance and manifesting are the rocket fuel. You have to combine both of them to truly live a life aligned with your purpose, soul and Universe.

How many times have you thought about an old friend and presto! Literally, minutes later you receive a message from them? Or… how many times have you found yourself talking about someone you haven't seen in years—then all of a sudden, you run into them at the grocery store?

These, my dearest, are all signs that you are in tune with the Universe — it's almost as if the moment you think about something or even speak of it, magically it appears. When you let your intuitive intelligence tap into the greater cosmic mind and surround you with positivity—magic happens! Hence why it is of great importance to cut your ties with energy vampires. You will notice a lot more things coming to fruition, random acts of kindness and that all your desires and wishes in life will come true.

The trick to manifestation is to visualise it into *being*. Create whatever you desire into being. The mind cannot tell the difference between what is real and what is not real and thus by having a daily or weekly practice of visualisation, you are in fact training your mind to believe it already exists. Your mind can go off on a wander but if you can practice daily intentions, you will be setting yourself up for success because the mind will act on them.

The purpose of setting a daily intention is one of the best ways to keep you on track with meeting your goals and achieving the level of happiness you desire. Intentions provide you with the focus you need to progress towards what you want to achieve, and they can show you what to say *"no"* to and thus save time and energy for what matters most. They can be small intentions such as.

- Today I am going to listen to more
- Today I will be more conscious of my thoughts
- Today I am going to be more present with what is (*practising mindfulness*)
- Today I will practice acceptance

Successful people use the power of visualisation; their motto is – to *visualise and materialise* – from imagination to reality. Even our friend Albert Einstein says – "everything is energy and that's all there is to it." Match the frequency of the reality you want... and you cannot help but get that reality. It can be no other way. This is not philosophy or an opinion, it is physics.

Using your present as the future...

So, we know the mind cannot distinguish between past, present, and future; therefore, the mind cannot tell time. The mind cannot tell the difference between what is real and imagined. The mind cannot differentiate between what is right or wrong, positive, or negative. The mind is a wonderful servant but a terrible master...

With these facts in mind, imagine what it would look and feel like if we were able to activate our emotions ahead of time. What if our brain created pictures of what our future would look like? Now that's magic!

Well, it can. The technique is called future pacing. And it can be life-changing. The list of famous, successful leaders and entrepreneurs that use this trick is a mile long. They too engage in future pacing, placing themselves in situations as if they had already taken place.

Okay, then, how do you start? Firstly, it's important to identify and acknowledge where you are right now. For example, if you are working in a corporation but you have this idea that you want to create your own product and launch into a completely new market, you must consider a few aspects.

And the way to do that is by having an end vision in mind.

- What does the end product look like?
- What does it feel like?
- What are your customers saying about your product?
- What are you thinking and feeling at the time?
- What is it that you want to change in particular?

Tapping into your emotions is of essence...

The second part is to project those heightened emotions into the future. It's the reason why we call the process future pacing. All you must do is decide on an end date, then close your eyes and let your emotions elevate. Allow the excitement, the butterflies, and the abundance to flow in. Imagine the experience as if it is taking place right now.

Then, project yourself into the future and allow your emotions to explode with joy, gratitude, and pride, right then and there. Time is just an illusion. When you are experimenting with future pacing, it doesn't have to be years in advance.

You can future pace months ahead of time if you want to practise an interview for a new career move. You can future pace two weeks ahead of time before a presentation. Or anytime that resonates with you to influence an outcome. When rehearsing, the key word here is *'imagining'* what it would be like to have that as if you were in that very position.

The process of imagining can even be compared to when you have a crush on someone–you think happily about them, daydreaming about the two of you together and the future scenarios you may share. You don't worry about whether the relationship is likely to occur in these moments, you just allow the mind to enjoy the thought of it.

In addition, gratitude and acknowledgement are critical to recognise when you have achieved the very thing you set out to achieve.

Your creative brain will tell your story...

Future pacing takes place in our prefrontal cortex – the leadership part of our brain. When we can imagine our future with augmented emotions, our brain is firing new neurons. We also know that neurons that fire together, wire together, creating new patterns.

Each time we do that, it's like building muscle. We are changing our minds and transforming our brains. If we keep imagining, thinking, and feeling our future, it will become our reality. When we are feeling the emotions of our future, our body receives chemical signals of these emotions telling our body—which is our unconscious mind—that the event has already taken shape.

It is a conscious practice because our default brain always has negative biases emerge in a blink of an eye. So, by practising a daily mental rehearsal, we are in fact creating new neural pathways in the *'present'* moment that will take us into the future.

Your thoughts can heal you from the inside out...

Science is proving that our body's ability to heal and repair itself greatly is affected by our beliefs, thoughts, emotions, and intentions, for they have a profound vibrational effect on our continually evolving genetic code.

We are the programmers of the code. DNA activation is our software upgrade. Dr Bruce Lipton talks about epigenetics, where he explains that the environment signals our genes and the end product from an experience in the environment is an *'emotion'*.

Therefore, if we embrace our emotions ahead of the environment, we are signalling the gene ahead of the environment. Genes make proteins that are responsible for the structure and function of our body. If we do our mental rehearsal well, we will reap the physical benefits and embody our future before it's actually manifested.

For that reason, it's important to understand that, if we don't get what we want straight away, we create a *'lack'* emotion and keep reinforcing the absence of not having what we want. When we are not in possession of what we want out of life, we automatically experience this emotion of *'lack'* from not having the very thing we desire.

If we allow those negative emotions to take form, where we are manifesting through imagination, then we are creating more of that very thing we don't want. As a result, it keeps us stuck in the past.

Don't lose your present to your past...

Our past is the biggest challenge we face—we can get stuck in the *'lack'* that we experience on a daily basis, moving us further away from our future creations. When we have our emotions triggered, we bring our past into our present and then hang on to it, and we are then projecting our past misfortunes into our future.

As a result, we can't see the future through the eyes or windows of our past. When we are in a state of *'lack'*, we give up trying for the future and hope that someone or something will come and rescue us.

You have the power to change. Only you can make a difference. Only you can make the change. You can create your future right now by tapping into your emotions and keeping the vision alive until it shows up. This means ... you must give up the life you have, to get to the life that's waiting for you.

You have to feel it to heal it...

In chapter one we took a deep dive into *'triggers'*, where we learned that once we became aware of our triggers—we were then able to give them a name (*label them*) and thus were able to discipline them before they got out of control. We then have a choice of what to do with them. Are we going to respond or react to our triggers?

Two very different outcomes are present. To react is to allow one to immerse themselves in the depth of the bubbling emotions. And to respond is to create enough space between the stimulus (*the trigger*) to then decide our best way forward. It takes practice to pause in between your trigger and response, but I promise you with practice, this is a game-changer.

Emotions are usually caused by triggers. Making long-lasting change requires us to break these emotional states down into bite-sized chunks. And then, once we understand the emotional triggers in our lives, we can reverse engineer the whole process and get to the root of everything that holds us back. If we don't make the necessary changes at the source, then we can only make superficial changes—and this kind of change is only temporary.

Emotions—particularly those that appear to us as *'instinctive'* and which are often negative, are usually caused by triggers. For example:

- My children are misbehaving so I get angry and start yelling at them.
- I am stuck in peak-hour traffic. I may be late for work, and I begin to feel stressed.
- My doctor has ordered some blood tests. I am very nervous—I have catastrophic thoughts about my health, and I can't focus on anything else.

How we feel affects how we act...

There is a strong link between the way we feel and the way we act or react. Often the behaviour is unconscious and therefore we are not aware of it until we examine ourselves very closely. Or... until we get independent feedback from someone who can help us to shed light on our blind spots.

For example, if you feel frustrated, your usual behaviour might be to yell and scream. As a result of this behaviour, your guilt might set in and then you find yourself overspending on your children or your spouse to compensate for your actions.

Do you see how this has the potential to become a vicious cycle? This is a trap that becomes almost impossible for all parties involved to free themselves of because they get used to *'relating'* in this way. It is just one example of how relationships can then go from being open, honest, and rewarding, to highly reactive, volatile, and dysfunctional.

When we are in a highly emotional state, we can unconsciously magnify, jump to conclusions, or blame others. In order to avoid this highly charged and over-stimulated emotional behaviour that's rash and often harmful, we need to become more conscious of our thoughts and feelings and how we communicate with ourselves.

It is possible, depending on its focus, for the mind to distort, delete or generalise information to align with our negative and limiting beliefs.

Give your emotions a daily workout...

Working with your emotions on a daily basis is one way that you can begin to regulate them and harness their power. You can then use your emotions as a guide or roadmap to help you navigate the changes you want to make in your life. Sounds simple, doesn't it? But you'd be surprised. We live in such a fast-paced environment that many of us have difficulty finding time for self-reflection.

So, here's the challenge... Spend five minutes a day with yourself. Go somewhere quiet, where you won't be disturbed. Evaluate. Go over the problem, situation or thought in your mind. Be still and listen to yourself. Take your journal and check in—breathe, spend a moment looking at your day, the events that transpired, the people you met, and most importantly—objectively think about how you responded to these and what you felt when you were *'in the moment'*.

Think about things that gave you heightened emotions—that is, those things that made you angry, sad, and disappointed. Why? Writing out your emotions in this way helps give you insight into where and why they are present. It also helps you to distinguish between similar feelings like anger and frustration. Knowing the difference is key.

Take your emotions dancing...

I'm a visual person so I like to make analogies. When emotions come up for me, this is what I do. In my head I put on my dancing shoes, turn up the stereo and take those emotions out on the dance floor. I hold them tight, and I ask them three questions:

- Why are you here?

- What am I to learn from you?
- What do I do with you?

Emotions need to be acknowledged. If you ignore them or repress them, they just come back ... with vengeance! But when I take them dancing, I am welcoming their presence. I am able to observe them objectively from all sides, as they twirl and whirl with me. I can spotlight, confront and challenge... and I am able to separate myself from the emotion, which is possibly the most important thing of all because it allows me to find perspective.

There are numerous benefits of doing this exercise on a daily basis:

- It will impact your well-being
- It will help you *'tune into'* your feelings
- It will help create a connection to the *'self'* – aligning the heart and the mind
- It will help unblock stagnant emotional energy that could be causing pain or even disease in your body.

Once you start to move the stale energy that is blocked in your body, you'll sense a cognitive shift that takes place too. This is the beginning of the wonderful change that is happening within you. And by being present, and ensuring that this work you're doing with your emotions has your full intention and attention—you can start to change your bad habits and move forward in a more positive direction, one that makes you feel like dancing. Every. Single. Day.

Label your emotions...

Over time, we have been conditioned to repress our emotions. As we were going through our development years, we were often told things like *"don't behave like that in public"* or *"bite your tongue."* Our parents would continuously scold us, saying *"stop crying right now, or else..."*, *"that's enough whining, young lady"* or *"I've had it with you, who do you think you are?"*

You can imagine that the *'don't'* list could have taken up this whole page. By repressing our emotions, we have buried them deeply in that greater part of our unconscious mind. We have pushed them so far down that we wouldn't dare allow them to pop their heads up.

That's the reason we suffer so very much from our emotions. We resist. We don't allow them to have a voice. We don't allow these particular emotions to be heard and felt. Consequently, they build up. Then, just like an innocent child who wants to be heard, we will have an out-of-control, emotional burst because we are constantly pushing them away from us.

Suppressing emotions creates blockages in our physiology...

Our body stores our unresolved emotions, to the point where they can cause physical pain. For those that would like to really deep dive into this topic, there is a great book by Evette Rose called Metaphysical Anatomy, which speaks about the connection between mind and body.

We now know the damage we can create by hanging on to our emotions from a physical standpoint. Nevertheless, when we hold on to our repressed trauma, it can also *'freeze'* our personality.

Any significant emotional event can keep us *'stuck'* in a time warp. When this emotion gets triggered, we bring that memory into the *'now'*. With our present eyes, state, and emotion, we add to that memory. In turn, it becomes our personality.

Now, I am not saying to tell everyone your secrets. What I am sharing with you is that if we do not deal with any traumatic experience, it will respond exactly as if we are going through the experience over and over again.

Therefore, it is critical to resolving what you need to resolve today. You have to stop repressing the memory and allow yourself to reveal these repeating patterns that decide how you show up.

The pursuit of illness for secondary gain...

Memories are social and contextual—they are shaped by your experiences. What you keep isolated is precisely what keeps you stuck. Your identity changes and continues to grow, but you are trapped as a child in some aspects of your personality. You see this in adults all the time. You find yourself scratching your head, wondering how this leader can react or respond in such a childish manner. Well, my friend, they are frozen in time.

Some like to be frozen. I know this one individual who wanted to be a highly successful entrepreneur and she had all the skills, talents, and know-how to become a very famous person.

However, after working with her for some months, it was very clear that she had a secondary gain. She wasn't prepared to heal herself from some trauma that kept her stuck into thinking she deserved no more than an average salary.

Once we really unpacked the secondary gain associated with hanging on to this trauma, she was able to release it. She let go of that regular fortnightly cheque, to go and create a business that paid her ten times more than before. And it all started with asking the right thought-provoking questions.

'What' versus 'Why'

Awareness is key for us to make a considerable change to what emotions we hold within ourselves. You can only do this by performing an internal investigation, by probing the deeper part of your mind without judgement. You will be amazed at the results, as a mini-investigation will reveal a recurring story or a theme.

Some thought-provoking questions you can ask yourself in the process are:

- What are the most consistent emotions that present on a regular basis?
- What can I learn from these emotions?
- What are my emotions trying to tell me?
- What do I look like when I resist my emotions?

Have you noticed that all the questions start with a *'what?'* I purposely stuck with that format because the *'what'* creates curiosity and probes the brain to come up with a constructive answer that uncovers the motivation of your emotions.

A *'what'* question will help you get a rational response, whereas a *'why'* question evokes an emotional response. With a *'why'* question, you can find yourself building a new blockbuster drama movie. Just think about when someone asks you *"why did you do it this way?"* Your automatic response is defensive.

The *'why'* question is connected to the limbic part of your brain, which is the emotional or *'heart'* centre. Don't get me wrong, it has a purpose. For example, if you want to get to the heart of a decision, a *'why'* question will reveal the thought process. On the other hand, a *'what'* question acts as a quick way of diffusing an emotional response or reaction.

If you can name it, you can tame it...

Overall, it is essential that you never make a permanent decision based on your temporary emotions. Instead, you must turn towards your emotions with acceptance. You must accept that they are there, identify and label them to take back the power they hold over you.

By labelling your emotion, you are pulling it out of your unconscious mind. Thus, you are allowing that leadership part of your brain – your prefrontal cortex – to change the meaning and loosen the boundaries of your emotions.

It's super easy:

1. Label your emotion: I am feeling _____.
2. Probe: What does my emotion want? What's getting in my way?
3. Find three alternative meanings to your emotion in order to get unstuck.
4. Even more importantly, you must realise the impermanence of your emotions. Although you may feel overwhelmed, you have to remember that this too shall pass.

The final piece is to let go of the need to control your emotions. You have to work with them and allow them to unfold, be heard and have a say. Then you can heal.

The Universe is always talking to you...

You don't know the signs until you get the signs until you look back and see them and then you go uuggghhh....... By allowing yourself to become aware and receptive to the signs of the Universe – this is where you dance with your emotions, allowing yourself to feel your way through life by utilising your intuitive intelligence.

Remember the trick is to live as if you already have it. So, what would you be saying? Where would you be hanging out? Who would you be speaking with? Do this with no attachments because you already have to believe you have it.

The more patient you are, the less 'attached' you are to a specific outcome, and the quicker you will get to what you want .... Remember, doubt equals resistance. And resistance, as I mentioned earlier, just slows the whole thing down!

When you feel frustration, impatience, or doubt creeping in, begin to practice gratitude. Gratitude brings you back to a place of abundance because it focuses on all the good things in your life. And remember, there's a grand plan. Your job is to enjoy the journey and trust that everything is working out. Gratitude turns what we have into enough.

Albert Einstein believed that the most important decision we need to make is whether we believe we live in a friendly Universe or a hostile one.

The Universe is a friendly place ...

Basically, it boils down to your beliefs. If you believe the Universe is friendly and that things, come to you easily and effortlessly, then you will be receptive and allow things to take shape. This is easier said than done, it takes practice, and it is an art and skill.

When you open yourself up to accepting all that there is, you are opening yourself up to the abundant Universe. As you let go of the need to control your life, control an outcome, or arrange your life how you think it should be, then guess what?

The Universe has your back, it brings you an abundance of prosperity and wealth. And it lines up not in some crazy haphazard way, but in a way, that suits you well, and is just the way you like it!

Gurus have long shared the idea that the cosmic blueprint that we are living in is a Universe of *'abundance'* and that it holds the building blocks to everything. The Universe is continuously expanding to cater to our every whim and we should not fear, as there is enough abundance for all of us and more.

The Universe is manifesting according to our will, but it can only deliver that which is seen as being called into existence by us. We need to seriously filter our thoughts and emotions in order to project what we want to manifest in our lives.

Intuition is real. Vibes are real. Energy doesn't lie. Tune it and trust your intuition, it will serve you well in life.

Chapter 6
Expand Your Consciousness Using Archetypes to Improve Your Understanding of Others...

"All the most powerful ideas in history go back to archetypes" –
Carl Jung

Since the beginning of humankind, all mythological stories have been based on archetypes. As fascinating characters that are linked to the human psyche, they reside within the collective unconscious of human beings all over the world.

Archetypes have a well-defined character that we can all resonate with in some way, shape or form and are able to identify through our personality traits.

Archetypes live and breathe in the DNA of every single human being. If only one would pause long enough to be present to connect with our beliefs, attitude, and behaviours—one could harness the power to connect to their archetypes and use them to make radical shifts in their life.

By working with our archetypes, we are creating steps to help us begin to use our heart, soul, and brain, to help increase our energy, self-esteem, clarity, and success as human beings. Much of this is about changing our perception ... said with a wink, it's possible, but it's not always easy.

Our dominant archetypes are always communicating to us by how we live our lives based on our perceptions of the world, or the meaning we give certain events, beliefs, decisions, and values.

Our emotions and self-programs are what we believe to be true about our world, our capabilities, and our limits. And changing these beliefs can take some time. That's why we have nothing to lose in borrowing somebody else's beliefs to help us move forward, and super-fast!

The more we understand the interconnectedness of archetypes and our inner world, the more we will learn about achieving emotional, mental, and physical well-being. Collectively, our growing personal understanding will help shift the global consciousness from instability and discord to balance, cooperation, and peace.

Feelings are just visitors, let them come and go...

Our thoughts are energy, and they don't just stay in our heads. When we have a thought, we announce it to the Universe, broadcasting our thoughts in every direction and they form around us like an invisible magnetic light.

Emotion is energy in motion and is our strongest form of energy. It is the magnetic force to our thoughts, connecting with like-minded atoms in our world and is what manifests our thoughts, our ideas, and beliefs into reality.

The amazing thing is that for the rest of our life, we are going to be surrounded by this magnetic energy field of light. It will constantly attract and repel things to us, just like the archetypes that we invite into our realm for different occasions.

So, how about deciding right now, to attract only the positive experience, and repel the negative ones? No matter how tough it sounds, it is possible. But only if we are willing to master our heart, mind, and energy!

And as I have alluded to in the previous chapters the first step is to understand that our emotions from past experiences get trapped in our bodies over time. This means these lower vibrations are still attracting more negative experiences, causing repetitive patterns, pain, or illnesses.

Even though a significant emotional experience may not actually be negative, the chemicals created in our brain from these trapped negative vibrations tend to make our mind perceive a neutral experience as 'negative'.

Self-awareness is the key to self-mastery...

Once we become more consciously aware of our emotional energy and vibration, we start to acknowledge the archetypal energy that is within us and around us.

Once we begin devoting more time to being conscious of which thoughts, feelings, or magnetic field we are sending out, we can find the positive within the negative and free our body from its energetic entrapment.

We all have the resources we need to cure and heal our emotional, mental, and physical well-being, all we have to do is to connect with the SELF and TRUST the SELF.

Osho explains that the cells that make up our body know instinctively what is nourishing and what is toxic. If we take a look at animals and plants, they communicate through vibration by sensing whether the energy is good for them or not.

We too have the same capabilities if only we stop, pause, and breathe a little to connect to our thoughts, feelings and our body that are all connected to our archetypes.

You see ... our *'higher self'*, that greater part of our mind, is where the truth lies. Eckhart Tolle explains it like this – *"we are the entire Universe, expressing ourselves as human for a little while."* Some people like to call it God, or a *'higher power'* or *'intuition'*. I'm going to call it the *'Universe'*. It is always speaking to us and sending us little messages just like the archetypes.

Abundance is something we tune into...

Essentially, the *'Universe'* is abundant. Scientists are only just beginning to understand its vast whereabouts and capabilities. It gives us exactly what we want or need at exactly the right time. Usually, though, as is the general human experience, we get in our own way... and we just don't end up receiving it. Or sometimes we don't listen properly, and we mix it up.

But something really beautiful happens when we start to pay attention. We find flow, and calm, and we become inspired because everything becomes alive again.

When we really pay attention, everything around us is our teacher. I like to think of our archetypes as our teachers with different knowledge and wisdom to share with us. All we have to do is pay attention and be conscious.

Our archetypes are always whispering to us and if we don't listen, we usually end up hearing from them, but after we have already done things the hard, long, arduous, or unpleasant way. The truth is that our archetype was ready to send us on a beautiful adventure before we got in the way of their instructions.

So, if we want to turn it around, we need to start paying attention to our energy. We are the only ones standing in the way of our happiness. In the grand scheme of things, we are all connected to each other through a higher sense of being. It's up to us to pay more attention to what's happening around us so we can guide ourselves to more fulfilling and positive adventures!

To go faster you must slow down...

As we deep dive into our mind, body, and energy, we will explore how to change the way we deal with our partners, family, teams, peers, and businesses as a leader. And... how to best deal with everyday stresses and strains that come from our increasingly fast-paced life.

Our underlying theme will be to *'slow down'* and reconnect with ourselves, tune into our power grids—our chakras, our archetypes—to gain more control over our mind, body, health, and energy connection. Only WE can control our future. We need to see that we belong to the collective unconscious mind and the archetypes that are the DNA code of our soul.

Through the understanding of how to harness the power of archetypes, one can grow abundantly and experience transformational change. Archetypes constitute the structure of the collective unconscious and are the energy guides that show us the way to our highest potential.

They will always be the fundamental units of the human mind that evoke a deep emotional and spiritual journey.

The archetype of Anima and Animus...

Carl Jung thought that the psyche was inherently an androgynous entity regardless of the physical gender, containing and embracing both the feminine (*Anima*) and masculine (*Animus*).

The Anima refers to the unconscious feminine dimension of a male, although men often forget or neglect to embrace their inner feminine side in fear of being criticised or ridiculed. But for men to step into a mature masculine role, they must go on an exploration and seek this inner divine feminine energy to unite with the other half of their soul.

When a man has connected with their feminine Anima they will display gentleness, patience, and compassion. However, when the feminine Anima is repressed within the man, it will often result in a negative expression of the Anima such as moodiness, gloominess, and sensitivity. Therefore, a man that has thwarted embodying their Anima will gravitate to the likes of hostility, ruthlessness, and coldness in their life approach.

Contrastingly, the Animus, otherwise known as the male element within the woman, is often silenced and suppressed due to traditional expectations that a woman must be nurturing and submissive. When the Animus is expressed, it can result in strength, assertiveness, and composure, however, when overextended one can reveal the negative traits of the Animus such as being argumentative, insensitive, and destructive.

Women that fall prey to these negative traits then fall victim to the '*crazy woman*' stereotype. Unfortunately, this then becomes a catalyst to further label and suppress women into believing they will appear '*too much*' when demonstrating assertiveness.

When our focus is on a principle of relatedness...

The Anima is the image a boy holds of his mother. Later in life, this is projected onto his relationships and the same can be said with the Animus is the image a girl holds of her father. Hence, it is of great importance to own our Anima and Animus. At some point we need to stop projecting our sh!t onto our partners and when we do, we experience a strong sense of ownership, accountability and responsibility. The integration of such archetypes will leave us with a sense of wholeness, happiness, and a life purpose. You can imagine the opposite of that when one does not integrate its very Anima and Animus.

To bring your hidden gems to light, invest some time with your earliest memories of your parents or primary caregivers and how you relate to them. It would be wise to grab your journal and reflect on the questions below. Do not judge yourself in this process. Simply allow your stream of consciousness and let it flow onto your pages.

- How do you feel about your parents and how do they feel about you?
- How do you relate to your parents and how do they relate to you?
- What did you like most about their relatedness to you?
- What did you like the least about their relatedness to you?
- If they had to say something to you what would that be?
- If you were to say something to them what would that be?

Now for the big question. Does the way you relate currently to others reflect the way your parents related to you or the views that they held? Food for thought. It may not come to mind in an instant but sit with the question long enough and the answer will come to you.

Your four most trusted allies...

We are about to wander through the labyrinth and demystify the archetypes and their Universal pattern of behaviours. Once discovered, they help individuals better understand themselves and others.

When we look back in history, the most powerful ideas go back to archetypes. The four primary archetypes influence how we relate to material power, how we respond to authority and how we make choices. These archetypal energies are neutral. They also symbolise our major life challenges and how we choose to survive.

The four archetypes are the Child, the Martyr, the Saboteur, and the Hustler. These four survival archetypes are programmed at an early age to keep us safe and small.

All are deeply involved in our most pressing challenges related to survival. They expose our different fears, vulnerabilities, and concerns that we need to confront and work through.

The way that we respond, react, and show up during challenging times will give us a hint on which one is more prominent, why we do what we do, and how we collaborate with others.

The light-hearted child loves to play…

We all have an inner child. Every child has had a very different upbringing and a unique experience. Some have undergone abandonment or trauma, while others have had time to grow out of their innocence. However, the adult or mature child that we are today has a craving for fun, play and to be light-hearted about life.

The child part of us doesn't want all the seriousness of adult responsibilities. The inner child is very much dependent on others to make decisions for them and anything that has to do with serious choices.

These child-like individuals strive for safety, freedom, connection, nurture, and loyalty. The child can be too afraid to speak up in a group or make decisions, so they contract and hold back.

Being a child that is heavily dependent on others, you are sometimes met with difficulty when it comes to responsibility. The lines are blurred. You can imagine how that shows up as an adult.

Martyrdom is only the beginning of personal boundaries...

The Martyr is a great lesson that lets you know that you are about to allow yourself to be victimised. This ally is always speaking through you. It's a matter of listening to the signs. By allowing the victimisation to take place, you will identify that you feel angry for allowing it to take place. Thus, you will take it out on others for personal gain.

Playing the victim means you are blaming others for your circumstances or disadvantages. It means you are always sharing stories of how others take advantage of you. Ultimately, it's only a pattern that is playing out. It is a pattern that is created by YOU.

Sometimes, this is how we receive attention. Being a victim is a common fear. It may have come from the very first time you didn't get what you wanted or needed as a child. Or you may have been punished for something you didn't do. You may have suppressed your outrage at the injustice because the victimiser was bigger and more powerful than you.

Therefore, as an adult, you may be afraid to stand up for yourself, or you may enjoy getting sympathy. The core issue of the Martyr is whether it's worth giving up your own sense of empowerment to avoid taking responsibility for your independence.

Imagine how much you would achieve if you stopped sabotaging...

The Saboteur may come across as a little negative because it is associated with deception. However, we can learn so much when we become an observer and see how we are actually sabotaging ourselves.

The pattern of the Saboteur is to protect you. Yes, to protect you, because you only get in the way of you due to your past experiences. This ally may show up in any area of your life, career, relationships or even success.

Remember, this is only a pattern because of fear. Fear of loss. Fear of control. Fear of showing up and being seen or being hurt.

The Saboteur's fears are all related to low self-esteem and self-worth. Consequently, it causes you to make choices that block your own empowerment and success.

Through it all, the Saboteur is calling out to you. It is seeking your attention to point out the areas in which you are getting in your way. Once you become aware of your Saboteur, you will hear and see the warnings loud and clear. Instead of being so destructive, you will stop repeating unwanted patterns that undermine you.

The trick is not to turn away or ignore it. You must lean into it. Face it. Make it your ally. Befriend it. Only then can you make sense of it.

The only cure for the struggle is to hustle...

We can learn so much from the Hustler. This is when we exchange our souls to get what we want or to have our needs met.

This ally engages lessons in negotiations of one's integrity due to fears of physical survival or for financial gain. It activates the unconscious attitude that is related to control and persuasion. Here, you have the capability of buying and selling the interests of others.

How this one shows up is that, for you to be accepted or approved, you sell out your ideas, give your talent away or allow others to take your precious time, but in exchange for something.

The lesson for this ally is to clarify our self-respect and self-esteem. We give our power away when we sell our ideas, compromise our integrity and financial gain. It clearly shows up in staying in a job or relationship that threatens our well-being for financial security.

Remember that we always have a choice in how we react and respond to our unconscious patterns. In other words, if we are the observer of our life, rather than being in it, blinded by unconscious behaviours, we can learn so much more about ourselves. As a result, we can grow, expand, and flourish.

For your own sake, practise being the observer of your life just for one day. Adopt a curious mindset, use your four trusted allies, and have the intention of discovering and learning about yourself. The more conscious you become about the unconscious patterns that are influencing your behaviours, the more likely that your choices and learnings will be empowering.

Honour and embrace your inner child...

Your inner child is that part of you that wants to have fun, be silly, indulge in creativity and not take life so seriously. We all have an inner child, it's that part of you that can be its most authentic self without caring what anyone thinks, feels, or says about you. The thing is that most of us do not connect with that aspect of ourselves and yet when one does, the experiences are quite profound.

As I am writing this paragraph, I am gazing at a photo that I have of myself at the age of 20 months. The purpose of my holding this photo is to be more conscious about the words I speak—meaning when I get a little lost in self-criticism, I look over at that little girl and ask, *"would you speak like that to her if she was standing right in front of you?"* The answer is always *"no!"* and I tell you what, I quickly change from being hard on myself to being compassionate and loving.

Your inner child is that part of you that wants to take risks, play, and fall. We can learn a tonne from children, they stand in their truth if they don't like something they will let you know and if they are angry, they let themselves feel the emotion. Not ever do you see a child let their cry out only to second guess themselves and ask, *"Was that cry too loud?" "What did people think of me?"* Or *"I should not have cried like that!"*

Healing your lost inner child...

> *"We don't stop playing because we grow old. We grow old because we stop playing"* –
> **George Bernard Shaw**.

Your inner child is the child that resides within you—and with it carries tremendous wisdom, intelligence, and insight but also profound pain. Therefore, inner child work is so transformational—it's a process of connecting, accepting, embracing, and healing your inner child so that you can experience joy, freedom, and bliss in all areas of life.

Unfortunately, this is not a hot topic—meaning it is not something you hear adults speak about and definitely not something that we are taught to do. If only we were to nurture this sacred part of ourselves. But instead, we repress its very existence and wonder why we are stuck or stunted emotionally, psychologically, and spiritually as adults.

The difference is now that you are an adult with a timeline of emotional experiences, you can use these events to gather a sense of what your inner child is asking of you. This is the shadow work that is of great importance because you will keep attracting people, experiences, and events to you until you attend to that wounded inner child of yours.

A fear of abandonment...

Let me bring it to life with one of my examples. If you were to glimpse down my timeline and look for the repeating significant emotional events that took place, it was very clear to me that *'abandonment'* was the recurring theme in my life. It began as early as 18 months old. I recall it as clear as the day after I invested some time into my inner child and the feeling of abandonment it grasped onto. I remember my parents left me with strangers because they had to go to work. This left me feeling confused as I did not understand why, and I continued to wonder what I had done wrong.

Fast-forward ahead of time, I'm an adult battling with a lack of self-worth, difficulty in trusting others and struggling with guilt and shame. When you start to observe your life and look for the repeating patterns, evidently you will start to notice what shadow or wounded aspect of yourself that you will need to integrate. Every time I found myself exhibiting people-pleasing tendencies, I knew right there this was a sign of *'abandonment'* that was playing out.

When I stopped people-pleasing... (*mind you I still at times find that I dance with it but definitely have improved over time*), those people were no longer in my life. When I included *'me'* in every decision where I stood in my truth, those people were no longer in my life. In fact, what was taking place was that I was healing the wounded parts of my inner child. When we are estranged from the child within, we are left with a feeling that something is missing.

Breaking through the cycle of suffering...

We hear it all the time. From a physical point of view, you have to work hard, you have to sweat... and you have to have a level of pain or discomfort to get what you want out of your physical body. If it doesn't challenge you, then it won't change you. Isn't that the truth?

But if it were that easy, we would all be doing it. However, we all resist change because it takes a lot of work, time, and energy. Change is an inside job. It's that saying that you hear all the time. If you want something that you've never had before, then you have to do something that you've never done before.

And that is you stepping out of your comfort zone. Just the other day, I was listening to a teacher, and she said something that truly stuck with me:

- You have to lean into the suffering.
- You have to learn from the suffering.
- You have to build a strong relationship with suffering.

Well, you can imagine my initial reaction. *"I don't think so ..."* But then it dawned on me. If I look back at all my suffering, each event or situation has been a pivot point or a radical shift in my life. No matter how painful it may have felt at the time, looking back on it now, it was my shadow, those disowned, repressed and unconscious patterns that wanted to be seen and heard so they could heal.

This my dearest is how we identify our shadow because the pain, the hurt and the suffering that we see in the world around us are often mirrored by our internal wounds, trauma, hurt and suffering. And this is how we find gold in our shadow.

The root of suffering is attachment...

Suffering is one of life's greatest teachers, and that suffering is the true training ground of self-transcendence. But the thing is this—we get to choose our suffering. We can choose one that creates meaning. And that helps us grow spiritually, emotionally, and mentally.

With this aspect in mind, why then do we label suffering, pain, anxiety, and stress as something bad? Neuroscience provides enough evidence to claim that our brain goes through cycles of suffering, only to avoid and escape suffering in ways that only perpetuate it.

We, as a race, are addicted to stress when we know that stress doesn't exist. We all perceive stress in different ways, and we all have different meanings of stress. Most of us thrive on a little stress to push us forward.

We get stuck in our ways of thinking, our ways of working, and our ways of reliving the past. We get addicted to our stories, our old programs, and our old patterns. All this is only to avoid suffering in the first place when we know that the deep work may hurt and that the suffering itself will lead to a new way of being.

There is never a quick fix. And even if there is, it will never be enough for us. However, we are satisfied, fulfilled and content when we work hard to achieve what we have accomplished. Think about it. A project you worked hard for. The sweat and hours you invested in your fitness. Even the timeless hours, tears, and persistence towards making a relationship work. It's the realisation of your grit that you stand proud of today with a smile on your face. You pushed through the suffering knowing that you were going to grow from it.

Hold on a minute, let's go back a couple of paragraphs. What did you mean by stress doesn't exist?

Stress is what you don't say...

Let me explain with a scenario so you get the picture. It's a Monday morning and you are at your desk typing away, as you have a deadline to meet. You need to get a proposal out before 11 am. Suddenly, a work colleague bursts into the room. Without excusing themselves, they rudely interrupt... while you are right in the middle of writing a proposal. In a very unpleasant tone, they say, *"can you get this done by this morning?"*

No *"please"*, no *"do you have the time?"* and no explanation as to why. Your stress levels will skyrocket just by sitting there and saying nothing. This is just one example that you will frequently encounter. There are countless others, like not standing in your truth by saying *"I am not happy"*, *"I am not fulfilled"* or *"I don't feel valued."*

Holding back information is far more stressful to the mind and body than saying it like it is. Another common way that we create our own stress is by saying *"yes"* to everyone. Each time you do something for someone else, you are leaving yourself out of the equation.

For instance, I know many of us—including myself in my younger days—used to always say *"yes"* to social invitations. After accepting to go out to dinner or a dance, I would then find myself racking my brain for excuses to get out of it. Naturally, I would then get annoyed because I should have been comfortable enough with saying *"no"* in the first place. By guiltily saying *"yes"* when you really wanted to say *"no"*, you end up feeling angry, frustrated, and stressed out. Basically, you create a massive amount of stress for yourself. Unnecessary stress. This is why boundaries are healthy and necessary!

The load doesn't break you down. It's the way you carry it...

The best way to acknowledge stress is to view it as an opportunity to learn and grow from the experience. When you catch yourself labelling an experience as stress, I encourage you to do a quick check-in with yourself.

Check if the stress is an internal or external driver. Maybe it's someone or something in your environment. If it is, what meaning are you giving this scenario? How can you give it a different meaning? If the driver is coming from inside, then do an internal audit or enquiry. Ask yourself *"what is this stress all about?"* and write what comes to mind. You will be pleasantly surprised that it may be something you have carried for quite some time that no longer serves you.

You are your greatest asset. By investing in yourself, you are actually rewiring your brain. Like any emotion, stress leaves an imprint on your brain, which allows you to better handle the next similar situation.

As one of my teachers always told us, remember the lessons, and forget the mistakes. If we can take learning from every failure, then we haven't failed at all. No matter how stressful an experience is, you can always learn something from it.

Growth through suffering...

If you think life is all about flowers, sunshine, and unicorns, then you are definitely on the wrong planet. On this planet, you can't escape from an unwanted experience.

Research has found this fascinating phenomenon called post-traumatic growth, which refers to the process of when a person experiences positive changes resulting from a major life crisis. According to the research, post-traumatic growth goes beyond resilience. By actively searching for the good in something terrible, a person can use adversity as a catalyst for advancing to a higher level of psychological functioning.

Richard Tedeschi, one of the psychologists who developed the post-traumatic growth theory, explains that *"People develop new understandings of themselves, the world they live in, how to relate to other people, the kind of future they might have and a better understanding of how to live life."*

In this context, we can better comprehend the progress that often comes after a traumatic event in our lives. But how do we deal with the overflow of emotions that arise throughout the process? And even more importantly, how do we tackle the fear that precedes authentic growth?

Reconnecting with your inner child...

Inner child work is revolutionary! By doing the inner child work, you are in fact reclaiming your power and have more vitality, enthusiasm, and joy for life than ever before. Most individuals that I have worked with say they find themselves more creative, innovative, spontaneous, energetic, buoyant, confident, blissful, and happy because they relate to what was once upon a time missing from their life. A connection to your inner child is connecting to that deeper part of your psyche—your heart and soul.

If this is not motivating enough for you and you are one of these individuals that are externally focused, maybe still on the people-pleasing train and still experience guilt for working on yourself, then this will be the kicker for you. When you do the inner child work, you are not only helping yourself, but you are also sending out ripples of change that will influence the whole of humanity as we know it. We are all part of the collective consciousness.

Your inner child is sacred work—and the impacts are very real. You may never quite know the butterfly effect or large-scale outcome of committing to such an adventure. The butterfly effect theory states that when a butterfly moves its wings somewhere in the world, it can cause a cyclone in another part of the world. And it has become, in modern times, a metaphor for the existence of seemingly insignificant moments that alter history and shape destiny.

Authenticity requires vulnerability...

The biggest booster when doing the inner child work is that you will get to see what is holding you back from being your authentic self. For example, if you were taught that it's not okay to have your own opinions... or if you were punished when trying to speak up or act differently, you can imagine the psychological impact that would have on a child. And not to mention the impact it has on you as an adult without your conscious awareness.

Often parents will verbally or physically tell their children off for having fun and being spontaneous because the child is either being too loud, emotional, or physical. People then wonder why now as an adult they don't know how to have fun, show emotions, or ask for physical attention.

Looking for the patterns will truly bring to light what sits in your shadow. The example of *'people-pleasing'* means that one does not speak nor stand in one's truth. It's easier not to have an opinion at all because honesty has consequences. As a recovering people-pleaser, standing in my truth and putting myself first was the biggest action required in order to heal my inner child and be my authentic self.

Comparison is the thief of happiness...

There are a few more patterns that you must keep an eye out for. For example, you may have had parents that *'compared'* you to your siblings, cousins, or any other important relationships within your life. As a child you may have had thoughts that you were not good enough, not smart enough or not important enough, leaving you with a comparison mindset. By constantly comparing yourself to others, you are in fact putting yourself, your skills and your talents down and therefore will not push yourself or strive to achieve your dreams.

Another pattern is if you are a *'rule-follower'*. As a child, you may have been acknowledged, recognised, or rewarded for following the rules. Then as an adult, you feel obliged to follow the rules, where you do what you think you should do, not always what you want to do. Allowing this pattern to continue may leave you not knowing what it is that you want out of life. You keep your ideas to yourself because you don't want to go against the grain and break the rules. And you find comfort in staying small and maintaining the status quo.

Another very common one is *'perfectionism'* where you feel the constant need to strive for perfection and nothing is ever good enough. This kind of mindset will hold you back from taking risks and will make you fear making mistakes. There are many patterns, these are just to name a few – once you acknowledge your repeating patterns, you will see them for what they truly are, the wounds from your inner child playing out that you need to heal.

The mirror is reflecting what you need to integrate...

The Universe is always reflecting to you what you need to learn. There is a coaching practice called the *'mirror work'* mentioned in previous chapters. It's a great technique when working with a coachee that holds strong beliefs about themselves that are no longer serving them.

As an example, if you are not happy with the external world whether that be a relationship, at work or with any kind of situation. The *'mirror work'* can help reflect that what is going on externally in your world, is a reflection of what is going on in your internal world. And by default, you are projecting that out into your environment for you to heal, integrate and make peace with.

If ever you are not happy with what is going on in your world, hold the mirror up and ask the question *"what is that an example of?"* See the things that bubble up for you. It's a potent exercise to connect with your inner child because soon enough, you will see these repeating patterns that are playing out. These patterns may be leaving you exhausted, confused, and not knowing what you want out of life.

It's a very simple process. All you have to do is sit in front of a mirror, somewhere where you will not be disturbed, with the intention of meeting your inner child. By setting an intention you are signalling to your subconscious and unconscious mind that you are ready to do the work. It's like setting a destination on your GPS—your unconscious mind will be guided by your very intention, making the session a purposeful one of that!

The inner child archetypes...

When you set the intention of meeting your inner child, be open to receiving the messages and don't judge what comes up for you. Just journal the thoughts, emotions, memories, and all that may come up from your inner child. Let your inner child know that you are ready to listen, give your inner child a voice, let your inner child know you are here for them, you love them... and they are safe to speak their truth.

There are many different inner child archetypes that may come to be exposed during this work. It may include the work of Caroline Myss where she talks about the presence of the inner child may come in the form of the wounded child, the abandoned child, the orphan child, the dependent child, the magical child, the innocent child, the nature child, to the divine child and eternal child. We will go deep into each archetype in this chapter.

There is also the work of Doctor LePera. For instance, we have the *'the caretaker'* which refers to someone who typically comes from co-dependent dynamics. This person gains a sense of identity and self-worth by neglecting their own needs. They believe that the only way to receive love is to cater to others and ignore their own needs.

Next, the *'the overachiever'* feels seen, heard, and valued through success and achievement. External validation is used to cope with low self-worth, believing the only way to receive love is through achievement.

Wounded inner child archetypes...

To *'the underachiever'* who keeps themselves small, unseen, and beneath their potential due to the fear of criticism or shame of failure. They take themselves out of the emotional game before it's ever played, believing the only way to receive love is to stay invisible.

To *'the rescuer'* that ferociously attempts to rescue those around them to heal from their own vulnerability, especially from their childhood. Others are viewed as helpless, incapable, and dependent, which allows them to derive their love and self-worth from being in a position of power. They believe the only way to receive love is to help others by focusing on their wants, needs and solving their problems.

To *'the life of the party'* that is always a happy and cheerful comedic person who never shows pain, weakness, or vulnerability. It's likely that this inner child was shamed for their emotional state. They believe the only way to feel okay and receive love is to make sure that everyone around them is happy.

To *'the 'yes' person'* who drops everything—and neglects all needs in the service of others. A person that likely modelled self-sacrifice in childhood and engaged in deep co-dependency patterns, much as the caretaker did. They believe that the only way to receive love is to be both good and selfless.

To *'the hero worshipper* or the person that needs to have a person or guru to follow. This pattern likely emerges from an inner child wound made by a caretaker who was perceived as superhuman, without faults. They believe that the only way to receive love is to reject their own needs and view others as a model to learn how to live.

Each type of inner child archetype has one thing in common—they were born from broken connections and unmet emotional needs. Then there are the 12 archetypes from psychologist Carl Jung.

The twelve-character Archetypes...

The Innocent archetype is subconsciously convinced that the better parts of life will somehow always find them. There's an understanding that life's hardest moments can be romanticised and pulled through with ease. As a child, the Innocent was spontaneous, trusting and overly dependent on others. There are journeys they wish to take but it is almost impossible for them to do so without their human safety net. Abandonment is high on their fear radar and avoiding that sinking feeling of being alone is a priority. The Innocent is blissfully unaware that the only person that can truly save them is themselves. This lesson is a quest they must eventually accept, discovering their flaws along the way.

Shadow side: The longer you live in denial, the less you are forced to accept the truth. Not everything will align with your ideal version of reality and that is okay. Accepting that you need independence will help you stop unknowingly hurting yourself and others. Trust your knowledge and critical thinking abilities, they will help form your new perspective.

The Orphan archetype is just that, a child still longing for parental presence, empathy, love, and acceptance. Life is simply a survival course and having well below-standard emotional needs satisfied is something they settle for. A person coined by street smarts, quick thinking, and little trust in others, it is no wonder they fear being used for others' gain. To overcome this issue, the Orphan must go through the developmental stages they missed as a child. There will be many emotional, self-victimising fits before they realise that their independence is a tool and not a harsh burden that unfairly targets them.

Shadow side: Surviving on your own has taken a toll and presents an ugly picture of the world. You feel bitter, as though the world owes you something. Someone has to take the blame for what you've been through. You can't help but blame your present setbacks on others and despite what you've overcome, you are now fragile and wounded. But even wounded soldiers still have to walk themselves back to base camp.

The Warrior – saving people is second nature to this archetype. The stereotype of being brave, tough, and self-sacrificing heavily applies here. While this may appear selfless, this person is quick to label others and perceive people as overly worth protecting or as pure evil and nothing more. Their actions reflect their entitlement to believing the world is a testing ground for their *'deep morals'*, when in fact, they are unbelievably shallow and empty people.

Shadow side: Choosing your battles is a battle within itself. It's time you take yourself out of your movie and understand that there are healthier, rational alternatives to achieving a sense of justice. Good and bad, winning and losing, are spectrums that all of us float along and gripping too tight to the better end will only harm yourself. Take a deep breath and know that not everything around you is a threat. Your friends certainly did not need you to defend their honour at that party you attended last week.

The Caregiver archetype is an altruist, an addict to the cycle of compassion, generosity, and comfort. Their caring nature is genuine but is also a major distraction. As a full-time employed carer would know, it is a 24/7 job and can leave little room for self-care. This person fears that selfishness will possess their personality and image if they let go of coddling others. The reality is that being a full-time *'parent'* will make whoever they are caring for, a full-time child. In the end, this will only cripple others and will destroy your self-worth. Remember, you cannot pour from an empty cup.

Shadow side: Despite attempting selflessness and reducing suffering in others, it is you that feels like the victim. You grow angry and helpless when people do not appreciate your care and expect that they owe you somehow. But no matter how many times they offer something in return, you will not take favours from others—forcing a co-dependent and manipulative relationship on both sides.

The Seeker archetype is on a mission to discover a more perfect part of themselves—a part that demonstrates their uniqueness, purpose and how this can amaze the world. They strive towards finding a new pathway, which often leads to issues with loneliness and perfectionism because they struggle to show gratitude and live in the present. It's a similar state to being a kid that hopes they are adopted and are actually a missing member of a royal family. You feel the people around you don't want the same greatness and exploration. However, it is crucial that the Seeker lets others in on their quest to find themselves, alongside managing their wild ambitions.

Shadow side: Narrow your ambitions to what you truly want and stop forcing yourself to be the billboard of success. You don't have to push others away and work tirelessly to improve yourself—it's often in those quiet moments with others where the greatest magic happens. Goals don't have to be extravagant in order to be worthy parts of your identity.

The Lover archetype refers to love in all forms, whether it's a relationship or love for a God or spirituality. While romance can be the best feeling in the world, it's also a place of immaturity, uncontrolled passion, and shallowness for a number of people. Rather than growing with whatever you love through intimacy, closure, pleasure or safety, this archetype treats love as a source of wholeness. It's what gets them up in the morning and is the main venture they look forward to pursuing. Doing anything to maintain the relationships they have formed in their lives is all too common for this archetype.

Shadow side: If you are a player, sex or relationship addict or a desperate lover who will settle for attention from anyone, you need to know that better love exists. Once you learn to love yourself and are content on your own, only then will you open the door to a calmer, free love that you have never encountered before. It will sweep you off your feet in the long term and feels like home.

The Destroyer archetype is rarely unseen in a fit of rage and causes unnecessary harm to themselves and others. They rebel against societal structures, including the ones they benefit from. Whenever an opportunity for them to grow arises, this is met with more hostility and dangerous, risky behaviour that may even threaten their life or others. In the hope to find peace and answers, they are not rebelling out of arrogance but rather to find a way to burn their feelings and energy.

Shadow side: Includes anything listed as a self-destructive behaviour such as binge eating, gambling, gaming, overspending, sabotaging relationships, and anything else that disrupts daily functioning, health, success, and functioning relationships.

The Creator archetype caters to all creative talents, ranging from fine art to the artistic side of engineering. People that fit this archetype typically overwhelm themselves with new projects, which can have both positive and negative effects depending on the individual. Creativity is a form of self-expression and helps them feel a sense of purpose in a world that's constantly moving but isn't really saying anything.

Shadow side: It's easy to become consumed with creative projects without realising your interest transitioning from an outlet to an aesthetic form of workaholism. The imagination is powerful too and it should only be used where it fits.

The Ruler archetype, if embraced productively, can be a powerful source of inspiration and accountability for those around them. They can be highly perceptive of others' motives and talents, making them perfect goal matchmakers if you will. However, their concern with order and structure can sometimes blind them into attempting to control others, believing they know what's best for them. Achieving the highest authority should never be the end goal. For example, if you are a parent, controlling your children too much will make them lose respect for you. They may then make poor choices to feel the freedom and control over their lives that they continue to take.

Shadow side: Getting your own way in every situation isn't all that you dream it to be. Whether you are an authority figure in a profession or embody one in your personal relationships, it always gets lonely at the top. The biggest lesson you can learn in life is that freedom comes from only worrying about the things you can control.

The Magician archetype values scientific knowledge and enjoys being always one step ahead. Their goal is to understand society and its people enough to influence everyone around them. Of course, this desire to change others can manifest in a positive or negative way. Cultivating hidden, misunderstood power of this magnitude may cause them to avoid understanding the self for its simplicity as the aim is to be something better.

Shadow side: With more knowledge comes more responsibility. You need to quit thinking about people in terms of possibilities and think about what is right. Talking down to yourself and others whenever you're not an expert in a situation results in a negative self-image.

The Sage archetype lives for the truth. The wisest of the archetypes, the Sage is highly analytical and seeks to live in a world that allows one to clearly evaluate their choices and learn from them. Transparency is important, although their attachment to it can induce the fear that anything traditionally unwise is automatically false. Letting go of dogma where necessary is something they need to work on. For example, the Sage may find it difficult to progress with developing political opinions.

Shadow side: To others, you often appear unfeeling, logical, judgmental, and as someone that does not take the time to understand others' emotional standpoints. Just because someone isn't doing what you believe is right, it doesn't mean it is not the truth in their mind.

The Fool archetype is the life of the party. They perceive life as one big game and adopt a fun, free-spirited approach to their work and relationships. However, when uninterested in the serious aspects of the world, they tend to resort to laziness and exhibit a lack of motivation. To the Fool, life is about how it makes you feel and if something doesn't make you feel good then there is no point in engaging with it.

Shadow side: You may have been told that you either never rest and get caught up in the excitement or that you are a *'homebody'* that needs to get out and accept responsibility.

By now if your head is spinning let me normalise it for you. It should be. We have covered quite a lot of different concepts in previous chapters from the different types of Imposter Syndromes to the inner critics, energy vampires, the variety of inner child archetypes to the Jungian archetypes.

The goal of these archetypes is to bring your shadow into the light. To shine more light onto those parts of ourselves that we deem as unacceptable, undesirable and unappreciated... *'aka'* bad!

The purpose of this work is to make the unconscious conscious to help you finally accept and feel your emotions become more conscious of the narratives that are holding you back and most importantly develop a greater understanding of yourself and others. Thus, reconnecting to your passions, dreams, and talents that you have swept under the rug, which by the way creates mountains of more shadow work for you to deal with.

Chapter 7
Embrace Your Shadow and Heal Your Wounded Self...

"When shadow work is neglected, the soul feels dry, brittle, like an empty vessel. Then, people suffer depression rather than embark on a fruitful descent. When shadow work is denied, the soul feels banished, exiled from its habitats in the wilds of nature. But when shadow work is attended to, the soul feels round, full, sated. When shadow work is invited into a life, the soul feels welcomed, alive in the gardens, aroused in passion, awake in sacred things." – **Connie Zweig** and **Steven Wolf**

We all struggle with judgement on a daily basis. Whether it's slow work colleagues, rude cashiers, or inconsiderate drivers, we are our own biggest critics and we tend to pass that judgement onto others.

Describing how things *"should"* or *"shouldn't"* be is the daily norm for most of us. Our mind is constantly shaking. It goes from calling something valuable to worthless, beautiful to ugly or good to bad. But judgement will always be a part of human nature. Imagine meeting someone for the first time with zero internal judgement about them, it would be quite an unnatural experience. We have been conditioned to judge as a protective mechanism that deems a person safe or unsafe.

Come to think of it, we often judge when we are out of our centre—when we are focused on external matters, when we compare ourselves to others and when we feel insecure. Most of the time we judge others when we feel judged ourselves.

Sigmund Freud explains overly judging people as a form of self-defence. Defending our delicate egos is our undesired thoughts, feelings, desires, and behaviours toward the people we are now judging. And that my friends, is shadow work right there. Rather than blaming external circumstances, let's take ownership and empower ourselves to feel greater comfort when around others.

We get a kick out of judging others because it makes us feel better than them. Whether it's an internal comment such as *"I would never go out with a hairdo like that"* to *"I wouldn't be wearing a short skirt with legs like that"* or *"I would never treat my children in a disrespectful manner in public like that"* ... we all have them. There should be no shame around your judgements, rather more curiosity as to *'why'* you do them in the first place.

Judgement creates limitations...

I don't know about you but when I become addicted to judgement, I feel drained, exhausted, and almost out of breath. If we have learned a thing or two from this book, it is that if we are sending out low vibrational judgemental frequencies... we are in fact attracting that very same energy our way. Judging a person does not define who they are—it defines who you are.

As it is known by now part of the shadow work is bringing more light into our dark side. It's about integrating those parts of ourselves that we have pushed away, repressed, or kept hidden from our conscious mind because once upon a time we were told not to express such talent, emotion or character leaving us puzzled with the belief that these were hindrances. And yet integrating these shadow aspects is the only way to make us whole.

If we are *'one'* with the Universe, then passing judgement on others is saying that we do not belong to this oneness—that we are separate from all that is... and that we are out of alignment with our true, loving nature. With all the turmoil and drama of our times, it has created more separation, segregation and estrangement which has become the norm.

When we feel attacked, our default position is to attack back as a way to defend ourselves and judge others for what they have done. Judgments confine us to a box. It restricts us from seeing our true potential, it blinds us from all the possibilities, and it limits us from being our authentic, brilliant selves.

Observe your judgement without judgement...

Judgement distracts us from our reality. When we judge, we often stop observing which then feeds lower vibrational frequencies such as anger, sadness, guilt, fear, and shame. So how do we let go of judgement? First and foremost, we must be conscious of our judgments. The way to do that is to *'observe'* our judgement without judging them as *'good'* or *'bad'* but more of keeping count on how many times a day we judge and what specifically we judge. Then how does it make you feel? Are your judgments helping, hindering, or hurting you?

We can't help to judge all that we are, do and have. Whether it's judging the way we look on a particular day, or whether we feel a certain way or even if we are having a good or bad day—and the list goes on. What about *'accepting'* all that is as is? Accepting that when we are feeling a certain way, we are able to feel the emotions and then let them go, rather than hanging on to them so ever tightly as if one's life depended on it—which creates resistance. What if we allow thoughts and emotions to pass through us like water flowing through a river stream with non-judgment and non-resistance?

This creates space between judgement and criteria, evaluations, or any internal assessments. The moment we practice acceptance of *'what is'* ... we dissipate, dissolve, deplete and so melt away the judgements. Yes. The judgement will vanish and disappear.

With a little persistence... one can experience the absence of judgement and find a sense of freedom. Why do we judge in the first place? What is the purpose of our judgements?

Judgement prevents us from seeing the good...

Everything we judge in others is something residing within us that we don't want to face. I know right, it's a hard pill to swallow. Spiritual teacher Gabrielle Bernstein once enlightened the class with a thought; the root cause of all judgement is when we think we are not good, worthy, or safe enough. It's a reliable little crutch when we feel insecure, hurt, or vulnerable.

Our judgement towards others makes us feel better, smarter, stronger, healthier, happier and any other positive feelings that fill in the blank. Judgments that cause emotional reactions are clues to help us find personal insight. These are the hot buttons we must pay attention to because they are hinting you the need to change. For example, just the other day at a conference I heard myself saying *"what a show-off!"* about an overly confident speaker. It dawned on me at that very moment I was placing a hard judgement on a complete stranger. I had no clue what their personality or beliefs hold, I only saw them forthright in their approach.

What possessed me to utter such words? What shadow aspect of myself was trying to get my attention? What needs of mine were not met and were screaming to be seen and heard? I then realised that I was judging that individual because I was not able to fully express myself. I was holding myself back from standing in my light when really, I was yearning to fully express my authentic self. You see when we accept and embrace all the glorious mess that we are, that others are, and that the world is... Now, this is a game-changer. Imagine if we were to *'accept'* all that is as if we have chosen every experience we encounter.

Working with 'what is' will miraculously transform your life...

The truth is this. When we judge others, we are really judging a disowned, deserted and denied part of our shadow. And the trick is this —every time you judge someone you reveal a part of yourself that needs healing. Just like when someone judges you, it isn't actually about you. It's about them and their own insecurities, limitations and needs.

Working with what you have is the quickest and best approach to start the transformation process. It will guide you to drop the judgement cycle because it is your ego getting a kick out of judging others—it's not you! Your ego loves to criticise and label others to keep you stuck in the old identity of who you think you should be.

We unconsciously do this all of the time. When we first meet someone, we think the sun shines out of their crown chakra. They can do no wrong in our eyes. This is when we are in a conscious relationship. However, over time when both parties drop their guard in the form of unconscious patterns, shadows, and egos—they can freely allow themselves to be seen.

Then we have the audacity to get angry, frustrated and annoyed with them for not being the person we thought they were because we gave them all of our power and realised, they were not the source of our happiness. We then project all of our lower vibrational frequencies including shame, guilt, grief and fear onto them. In other words, we project our sh!t onto them and begin the judgement cycle.

You see, a conscious relationship is when a couple is committed to their personal growth first, with the relationship following and courageously speaking their truth. To be vulnerable, to be of light and love.

Two things to keep in mind before we go any further. The best way to tame our ego is to become the *'observer'* of our life ... and the other is that happiness depends on ourselves, not others.

We judge others by their behaviour...

Stephen Covey said, *"we judge ourselves by our intentions and everyone else by their actions."* We automatically judge *'behaviour'* when the behaviour is not the person. The behaviour is what they are *'thinking'* and *'feeling'* therefore showing up as the behaviour.

This is so important for us to understand. All judgements, good, bad, or indifferent is not real, not true, and automatic. They are not a choice thing. This is how we have been conditioned over time. When we judge something as positive, good, or beautiful we are in fact giving more energy to the opposite reality. Yes, everything in life has its own polar opposite. Judgement has no benefits to us at all. If we judge something as good, positive, or perfect we are in fact creating a glass ceiling that begins to diminish what we could potentially receive. It limits us from receiving beyond our judgement.

You can't have a left without a right, an up without a down, success without failure, a good experience without a bad one and so on; it is a world of duality. There are two poles or opposites; the difference between the two extremes is called polarity. Within every failure, there is potential for success. Within every problem, there is potential for opportunities. Everything in life has an equal opposite. It is up to you as to what side you choose to focus on and experience.

There is no such thing as good or bad, big, or small—it is what it is. However, when you perceive it to be a certain way or the meaning you choose to give whatever is going on in your life, you are simply giving it a label. Labels truly limit us from seeing beyond the label.

Labels can be dangerous...

What you may label as a bad experience, I may label it as an opportunity and look at what I have learned from this experience so as to do it differently next time. If you did not experience sadness, you would not know what joy is, and without pain, you would not have pleasure. These polar opposites all work together for the greater good. You only need to understand this and appreciate the fact that they coexist.

Polar opposites may be:

- Good and bad
- Rich and poor
- Healthy and sick
- Sad and happy
- Pain and pleasure
- Failure and success
- Big and little
- Love and hate

Without one of these, the other doesn't exist. Since all things are relative, without failure you would never experience success. You can relate this to all areas of your life. Stop judging these aspects in your life and start recognising them for what they are. Failure and success are the same things on opposite poles. Within one is the potential for the other.

There is something very important that you need to understand when it comes to labels and their polar opposites. Our labels are unique to *'us'* and the meaning that we give them is going to be completely different from one another. For example, the meaning I have about love is completely different from the meaning that you have about love (*the same will apply to its polar opposite*).

Be mindful that labels can be dangerous. Labels create separation and they can shape more than your perception; they also change how you perceive people.

Potential for success...

How do you use this information to your advantage? As mentioned, within one is potential for the other. In every failure, there lies within it the potential for success. Once you acknowledge and recognise that one can't exist without the other and that they are the same thing—you need only turn your thoughts to the side of the spectrum you wish to experience.

With every dichotomy or opposite, it is really up to you as to where you focus. Just like a pendulum that has two dimensions, imagine any emotion. How long does it last?

It is with feelings as with the pendulum—they swing! Relentless! You may like one side more than the other. One day you may want to be:

- Alone
- With people
- In a relationship
- Single

- Working with an organisation
- Working for yourself

When you practice acceptance, you release resistance...

Acceptance is the opposite of resistance and will bring more of what you desire. If you can accept failure for what it is and move forward through learning, you will have the ability to accept success. If you resist failure, then you are putting your main focus on that failure. This then attracts more of it; you will never experience success.

The important part to get out of this information is that all things have their own polar opposites and without one, you would never experience the other, just as you learn that all things are relative. It is not good or bad; it is all in how you perceive it. Do not resist that which you do not desire. Accept it and move your thoughts to what you desire.

Do opposite dichotomies attract one another? For example, does an extrovert attract an introvert? Does a thinker attract a feeling individual? Or... does a structured individual attract an open, global-minded person? Perhaps they do. From my experience dichotomy opposites do not necessarily translate into harmony. However, the amount of evidence that I have seen with my own eyes shows that opposites combined appear to be a good match. Extroverts are energised more when talking about what they are thinking and feeling, and introverts are energised more when thinking about what they are thinking and feeling.

Nevertheless, natural differences exist in how extroverts and introverts perceive, process, and respond. For instance, extroverts require external affirmations to feel internally grounded and feel accepted; they are very driven by external influence, whereas introverts are completely the opposite.

The opportunity here is for you to have an open mind and ask yourself every day: *"What can I learn from this very experience?" "How can I chunk it up and find the balance between the two?"* Harmony, understanding and balance will all be welcomed into your life with open arms.

Dichotomies at work...

> *"I am the brightest light beaming from the darkest depths. A dichotomy, I am ... illumination."*

To say that I relate to Jaeda DeWalt's quote would be an understatement. I too have experienced some of the darkest moments, which have been my greatest lessons. From those very experiences, I am now aware, informed, and enlightened. However, if only I was aware of the dichotomies, the cycles and rhythms of life that are natural to our presence, the road may not have been so bumpy.

Just the other day, I heard, *"You want it so bad that you created the opposite, which is the fear of not getting it."* It struck me like lightning. And I'm certain that you can relate to it as well. Can you recall the very first time you fell in love, and you desired that person so much ... that you were terrified not to get them?

Or when you went for your very first job or that perfect career, after the interview you feared so much that you weren't successful ... because you wanted it so bad? I can relate to dichotomies in so many ways from my relationships. Instead of them going up and down, in and out, I now have found balance. I have found less extremity and fewer limitations because I now understand the Laws of Cycles and Rhythms. You can't stop them. They're like the sunset and the sunrise. It's all in how you dance with the rhythms and the meaning you give them. You only get back what ingredient combination you put in the mixing bowl.

Nothing exists without its opposite...

With every extremity, the opposite exists, and we invite it into our very existence. The thing here is to not get stuck on either side of the dichotomy, whether real or imagined. You hear it so often. Countless entrepreneurs, business owners and leaders say, *"we work really hard, but we play hard too!"* My response is always, *"how is that working out for you?"*

Guess what their answer is? *"It's not ... but I'm having trouble finding the balance."* It's not about finding the balance. It's about creating balance, so you don't have to be so extreme. It's so easy to get caught up in one side of the dichotomy. For example, those that know me know that I am a giver of my time and energy. To find the balance means allowing myself to receive more so as to feel more grateful and energetic.

There are dichotomies even in a leadership team. Some are soft and some are hard. Some are leaders and some are managers. Some are inspirational and some are de-motivators. Some are extreme and some are subtle. They all exist. The question is ... how do we make it work in a balanced way for ourselves?

Living with the cycles and rhythms...

You win some and you lose some. There is success and there is failure. There is triumph and there is disaster. Even our own physical body has a circadian rhythm. There are cycles and rhythms in everything that we do. They're in our environment, they're in nature and they're in life.

Sometimes we are super motivated and other times we are bored. We can go from loving to hating someone, from respecting to loathing. When we swing too much towards one side of the dichotomy, we are at our extreme point.

The secret is learning how to find balance amongst the chaos because the Law of Rhythm affects our health, our relationships, our economy, and lots more. Everything in the Universe has its own rhythm. The tides of the ocean come in and go out, but they don't stick to one side. They rise and fall.

This is what is called the cycle of life. There is always a reaction to every action. The balance then is not to react or respond to the extremity, but to remain neutral (*in your centre*). The one trick that has worked for me is to understand that they both exist and to not get caught up in the extremity of the emotions that come with the waves.

There is no end to this but death...

> *"The real question is not whether life exists after death. The real question is whether you are alive before death."* – **Osho**.

There are so many individuals that are so afraid of dying that they forget to live. Once again, it's learning not to get stuck on one. It's learning how to not get too excited or too down when things present themselves. We can't control all of the cycles and rhythms around us. But we can control how we react and respond to them. We can control our mindset. We can control our emotions. We can control the meanings we give to every scenario, situation, and opportunity at hand.

The more we learn to remain neutral and centred, the less we are going to experience mood swings. We can learn to be detached from an outcome, whether it's a relationship, a job, or an emotion. Otherwise, we will let the cycles and rhythms zap our time and energy to the point that we may stay stuck on one side of the dichotomy.

Instead, you can use your willpower to prevent yourself from getting too upset or too enthusiastic. You now understand that sometimes we have no control over some occurrences that play out in life, just like the tides of the ocean. It is up to us to decide whether or not we invest our time and energy in these highs and lows. We have the power to choose if we want to feel exhausted from going against the tide.

When you can master your emotions and control them before they control you. You will feel balanced, neutral, and not have to go through too many extremities. Don't allow the pendulum to swing too high to one side. If you remain centred, acceptance of all that was is and will be. Things will come naturally to you.

Live in a space of non-judgment...

"Be someone who judges no one!" – **Dr Wayne Dyer**.

To live a life of non-judgement is to stop judging yourself, your body, your relationships, your business, your finances—any and every part of your life. To do that one must be conscious, mindful, and present always. It is easier said than done but with practice, this is where the magic and changes happen. It is when you are standing in your light, love, and truth because you now know that judgements—all judgments diminish your receiving and are just the other side of the coin of a negative judgement.

You must become the *'observer'* of your life and notice every time you judge something as good, beautiful, or perfect—stop yourself and ask, *"Do I really want to diminish my receiving this positive judgement and in doing so give more energy to the opposite?"* Keep an eye out and spot your negative judgements because deep down inside of us we are projecting our *sh!t* out on others as a way to end our suffering. By projecting judgement onto others, we are in fact denying, rejecting and repressing our feelings—that can be any lower vibrational feelings such as shame, guilt, anger, or victimhood and in doing so this creates a perpetual motion of more shame, guilt, and anger for not allowing ourselves to experience such emotions... and then riddled with guilt for projecting our *sh!t* on to others.

Here is the reason why you must practice non-judgement! Judgement is the number one reason we feel blocked, unhappy, pessimistic, alone and separate from who we truly are—a being of light, love, and truth. When we feel separate from who we truly are, we feel less than others, not good enough and not worthy enough. We use judgement to protect ourselves from exposing our deepest pain, wounds, and trauma.

I do not follow a religion, but I did go to a Catholic school, and I remember a chapter from the bible that Jesus said: *"Don't judge others, and God won't judge you. Don't be hard on others, and God won't be hard on you. Forgive others, and God will forgive you."* In other words, non-judgement is not a new fad, the practice of non-judgment has been around for a very long time.

Negative judgments create negative experiences...

Get this! Whenever you judge your body—you create separation and eliminate receiving from your body. Whenever you judge someone—you create separation and eliminate receiving from you and that person. Whenever you judge yourself—you create separation and eliminate receiving from yourself. And yet we are all too quick to pass judgement and too slow to self-reflect. Because when you judge you do not come from a place of love and that is what causes the separation to begin with. No wonder we feel so lost most of the time, not knowing from one day to the next who or what we are.

Any judgement you think you are having with anything, or anyone is actually a judgement of the self. Judgement is not awareness. Judgement actually cuts off your awareness, limits your possibilities and disempowers you from knowing that your choice and contribution change everything. Some judgements are harder than others to let go of... especially if you have had the same repeating judgement for donkey years. Some may feel especially difficult or even impossible, but it can be done with time and love.

Whatever we resent or dislike in another person is a reflection of something we dislike in ourselves, or it is a representation of deep pain, wound or trauma we are unwilling to heal. Often other people trigger our wounds. We judge them when this happens instead of accepting that the discomfort is really about us.

Judgement is made of resistance and creates resistance...

Love heals everything! Love is all there is. When you come from a place of love, judgements cease to exist. Whenever you find yourself judging, pop your rose-coloured glasses on and be more compassionate to yourself and the other person. When you come from a place of the heart, you project more of that into your environment because love, compassion and all the kindness high vibrational frequencies are the antidotes to judgement.

It takes presence. It takes consciousness. It takes you to be mindful and always be in your centre because when you don't, this is where you get yourself into trouble. This is where we are just projecting our old stories, old experiences... and old belief systems into our current circumstances all the time. We drag the past into the present unconsciously and get caught in a judgement loop.

But when you surrender to what you know and let go of what you know —you will be sure to find more. Surrendering is an active space because you are walking into every situation with the *'not knowing'*. This allows you to discover openly and unbiasedly what is truly out there.

Let's use a rose for example. You know what a rose looks like. You know what a rose feels like, and you know what a rose smells like. By the very fact that you think you know, you are closing yourself to other opportunities, possibilities, and insights. Imagine looking at a rose and surrendering to what you think you know. Now, look at it for the first time— letting go of all your knowing and then seeing what you will discover.

Surrendering and letting go of the knowing...

You can use this same approach with anything and anyone. Use the knowing approach with a partner, a loved one or a family member as an example... you may think you know everything about them and that in itself is closing you off from learning more about them.

But what if you were to practise *'not knowing'* with everyone and everything around you? What if you were to approach them as if it was for the first time? You would be delighted and sure to find out more about them. It's your knowledge that is getting in the way of you learning or discovering any further characteristics, emotions or any other vibrational frequencies that may reside within that individual.

Surrendering is to let go of all-knowing, it is to let go of all expectations by keeping an open, alert, and curious mind as if you have no idea what is going to happen next. A surprise reveals itself and is the greatest, most unexpected gift of true adventure. The kind of adventure where it wouldn't even matter leaving your old life behind because the present moment triumphs over it any day.

Once you accept that everything in life is your teacher, that is when the healing really takes place. And you know what? You then get to choose. We always have a choice that is the *'free will'* that we came here to experience. We can experience the freedom that we dream about when we stop dragging the past into the present. When we stop living in the past and when we drop all judgement and come from a place of love. Love is the great miracle cure. Yes, loving yourself works miracles in your life. True love is the ability to love without judgement, expectation, and condition.

Our love flows unconditionally when we release resistance...

Now we understand that whenever we are judging, we are resisting love because we are protecting ourselves from not receiving it in return. Yet we are constantly screaming for love. It all sounds so counteractive, right?

Any pain we ever experience, whether it is emotionally, mentally, or physically, is screaming to escape. Instead, we want to free ourselves from such pain. Well, judgement acts in the same manner. When we become the observer and lovingly witness our judgement, then it can be simple to free ourselves from this pattern.

So, the next time someone places blame for wrongdoings, it's because they are doing it to themselves. All judgement is self-judgement! So, when someone judges your intelligence, looks, or quirks, they are in fact saying they don't like themselves.

If you are judging someone else, it is your own self-judgment that is automatically being projected from you. If someone is in the judgment of you, it is simply their self-judgment that is automatically being projected onto you. It's simply all about projection.

Not having the urge to defend yourself is real peace...

When you do not resist, repel, refuse, defend, fight, oppose or align with anyone's judgments—their judgments of themselves will begin to be invalidated and return to love. Yes! It is we that keep the judgement loop alive and spinning out of control. The only way to not have people judge you is to have you not judge you. Doesn't this blow your mind? Remember we are our own worst enemies, critics and judgement bully. Everyone around you, especially those that judge you, are a thousand times worse on themselves. Therefore, it is of great importance not to fight back against what has been dished out to you but do the opposite.

The biggest etheric slap was the realisation that I was creating my own pain and the funny thing is this—we keep forgetting that we are multi-dimensional beings and that we are part of the collective. And that everything we speak about, think, feel, or judge—we are in fact broadcasting this information out into the judgement reality only to attract more of its kind.

In other words, if you identify with any form of judgment, whether self-inflicted, self-judgment or associating with any form of judgment—you are in fact connecting to the collective consciousness of that judgment reality. For example, if you judge yourself by saying something like *"I am not smart enough!"* you are indeed tuning yourself into that broadband frequency or calling forward a vibrational frequency match. Then you walk around as if you own it—when in reality you are just automatically connecting with other people who are having similar judgments.

Love is the absence of judgement...

By being humble and non-judgemental, we can create peace. When we are in non-judgment, we can hold a space of infinite possibilities that allows something to show up that is greater than anything we can currently imagine. How do you know whether you are in judgement or awareness? Awareness changes expand, and shifts easily, whereas judgement makes you fight hard to hold onto it.

It's super important to pay attention to your ego. When you are in a place of judgement and blame, you know it's your ego that identifies with opinions, beliefs and what is called your false self. When you embark on shadow work, your ego will work overtime to create blame and drama to avoid you facing your demons. This is the drama triangle that the majority of us are not aware of, but it exists. In fact, this is the greatest diversionary tactic that exists!

Drama does not just walk into your life! Life is way too big... and time is way too short to get caught up in it. Gossip and passive-aggressive antics do not just come waltzing through your door. You either create the drama, invite the drama, or associate with the drama.

And there are some individuals who absolutely thrive on drama, seriously, they go fishing for it. To them, life seems boring unless there is some sort of action for them to dive into and get their hands dirty.

But ... a drama queen cannot exist without an audience! So, the trick is to ignore them completely, do not get involved... the less you feed the cycle ... the less you will see it expand. If only we could understand how unhealthy this behaviour is... we would not give it our time, or energy.

You can spot a drama queen from a mile away. They don't mind their business, they are constantly in your lane—and they push boundaries, having no level of self-awareness or limits. But creating drama for the sake of it is to seek validation from others. And this is never fulfilling. Self-love is the only kind of stable validation. Drama queens don't understand this, and so they perpetuate the attention, time and time again. It can be exhausting for all involved, even when you're only witnessing it.

Don't play the victim to circumstances you created…

Stephen Karpman created the drama triangle, which refers to a social model of human interaction. The model is used in psychotherapy or more specifically in transactional analysis. According to Karpman, anytime we don't take responsibility for how we feel, think and act, we fall into three characters that make up the drama triangle. And when we fall into the triangle, we are not facing nor leaning in towards ourselves. We are not even aware of the consequences we have on others, and we allow these states to play out and jeopardise important relationships.

The roles of the drama triangle are the victim, the persecutor, and the rescuer. Let's first take a look at the *'victim'* where they may make statements like *"it's all your fault"* *"I was forced to do it"* or *"things will never change, just my luck!"* The victim role comes across as needy, no one loves me, dependent on others, as a martyr or feeling abandoned or rejected in some way.

Sometimes a victim will play out the victim when they feel they don't get enough attention. This can come from their imprinting years, where they may have felt abandoned, unloved, and not valued. And as a child, behaving like the victim (*poor me*) got them the attention they were seeking, and this cycle may have never gone away.

The silent treatment is a killer of friendship…

The victim very much plays out the martyr, allowing them to use the whole guilt trip in order to gain sympathy. Quite often the victim feels helpless and trapped, seeing no way out of their powerlessness.

Another typical victim trait is staying in an unhealthy relationship where they find they can't trust their partner or themselves. They have this mindset that this is all they deserve and get upset with the smallest things. In a relationship, they know how to play the silent treatment, where they withdraw and refuse to communicate. And we all know too well that the silent treatment never solves problems ... it only makes them worse. Without communication there is no relationship—communication is the heart of every relationship.

Staying in this *'victim'* mindset is completely destructive. It can lead to feeling overwhelmed, oppressed, or depressed. Therefore, it is crucial in these situations, to ask one important question like *"what might be my opportunity to face, change, or do differently in this situation?"* Because if you don't stand up, you will be stuck in that never-ending tower.

People-pleasing hides the real you…

The other role that plays out in the drama triangle is the *'rescuer'*. This is when one person goes out of their way to please others, going above and beyond anyone's expectations. They often say *"yes"* and do things that they don't really want to do. Sometimes the rescuer lives in denial saying something like *"what me? I don't have problems!"* They walk around life saying that other people need help more than they do and forever make up excuses for why others behave a certain way. For what it's worth, I can relate to this style, big time!

People-pleasers (*a rescuer*) are always seeking how to make others happy or make things better for others. In their eyes, it is much more important to meet the needs of others than their own needs. But really when you look at the rescuer with a magnifying glass, what you see is what they do for others. In doing so they come across like they are taking control of situations, calm in a crisis, dependable, and helpful. But often, these situations really don't need their attention in the first place because in getting involved in other people's drama, they are avoiding the *'self'*.

The important question here is *"what am I avoiding?"* If this is you, it is time for you to deal with your sh!t. Putting others before your needs means that you are ignoring something that you need to lean into.

The tongue is a small thing but what enormous damage it can do...

The final character in the drama triangle is the *'persecutor'*. This is someone who puts people down and therefore goes one-up. Sometimes they can be mean, aggressive and a bully. Quite often the persecutor acts out of anger, resentment, revenge, or a sense of entitlement. Some statements that may come flying out of their mouth may be *"you are ruining my life!"* or *"I told you this would never work, dummy!"* or *"you are such a jerk, stay out of my way."* They are big meanies. And nothing is ever good enough for them.

Persecutors think that they are superior ... They get frustrated because they think everyone should think or be like them. They always need to be in total control of any situation, and so they come across as overbearing, and demanding, with a *'do it my way, or get on the highway'* attitude. And they can be sneaky and manipulative to get their own way. But underneath all of that is shame, fear and hurt. This once again is something that took place in their imprinting development phase, and if it plays out in adulthood, it has clearly not been dealt with. But once the persecutor can get to the root cause of their anger, they will start coming across in a more loving, respectful way.

As we unpack each one of these characters in the drama triangle, you can see how they can actually play out in relationships. When one is the persecutor, the other can be the victim and then the third could jump in as the rescuer to sort out the drama.

We attract what we are ready for...

Of course, nothing is ever black and white either, and we may find ourselves very strongly in one of these roles, or sometimes in others, depending on what we're dealing with in our lives. There's a little part of each role in all of us and we're each equally capable of playing them out.

But first and foremost, to grow and be our very best selves, we need to be conscious of what we're doing—how we're behaving, and why we're reacting. It's not as simple as thinking your *'sh!t'* is ever crossed off your list either – it has a habit of playing out over and over, even when you know that you recognise it, and even when you thought you'd faced it. This is not a bad thing—being conscious of who we are, what makes us tick and how we relate with others is a lifelong journey. We are richer for every experience that makes us sit up and look at ourselves.

But this is why it is so important to seek time. Alone time to invest in ourselves and see patterns at play. The drama triangle does not have to be the *'Bermuda Triangle'* into which you disappear and can't get out. If you invest time in yourself, you can hone your radar to see the triangle in the distance. And then you can avoid it altogether.

Spiritual bypassing to avoid dealing with unresolved wounds…

> *"Spiritual bypassing is a tendency to use spiritual ideas and practices to sidestep or avoid facing unresolved emotional issues, psychological wounds and unfinished development tasks"* –
> **John Welwood**.

Spirituality is an experience that creates a system of personal beliefs when searching for the meaning of life. It's a way of dealing with everyday challenges in life and connecting with something bigger than us. Being spiritual can mean different things to different people.

But when we use these practices and beliefs to ward off personal, emotional or to belittle basic needs, feelings, and development tasks—then this is spiritual bypassing at its finest. It means you are avoiding dealing with painful *'unfinished business' and are* living in denial as if everything is dandy!

Believe it or not, we all do it! So, let's normalise it. Spiritual bypassing is a normal process of suppressing, denying, abolishing and eliminating the shadow self or that dark side that resides within you… and masking it with sparkly, feel-good glitter bandages. Although we know all too well that by repressing the inevitable—the very thing that we must work with will only increase its power. When we stop resisting with what is —the struggle stops.

When we are tuned in, tapped in and aware of our body's defence mechanism, then we are awake, conscious, and mindful of its very presence. Once we are cognizant of its very existence, then we know we are seeking to use spiritual ideas to turn away from any unresolved grief, pain, trauma, and issues.

We all use spiritual bypassing to avoid dealing with painful feelings, unresolved wounds, and developmental needs. Since it is an unconscious act it's so pervasive that it goes largely unnoticed.

With the avoidance of pain, we lose the healing too…

Yep. It's a state of avoidance and thus a state of resistance. You can avoid reality, but you cannot avoid the consequences of avoiding reality. Avoidance doesn't solve anything; it merely serves as a temporary pacifier. Laing said, *"pain in this life is not avoidable but the pain we create avoiding pain is avoidable."*

When we are sidestepping or avoiding our problems, our spiritual bypassing language kicks in to avoid dealing with what you may have labelled as deep psychological issues. When we do such an act, we are masking and overlooking any emotionally unfinished business! In other words, we are covering up what we need to heal. Instead of allowing lower vibrational frequencies to envelope our very being with negative connotations—we do the opposite. We approach life with *'positivity'* on steroids and instead of dealing with what is really going on within us, we turn our focus externally to avoid the healing to take place.

If you can relate to any of the below statements, you know you are spiritual bypassing by avoiding action to justify the agony, adversity and anguish you are feeling.

- Everything happens for a reason
- It is what it is
- It was a blessing in disguise
- It was for the best anyway

In reality, we are just making it easier for us to digest what is taking place, making it easier for us to accept things as if there was some divine intervention taking place as part of our spiritual growth. Almost as if it is inevitable that these events were meant to take place for our learning. But what if we were to sit with our pain in order to process it and not repress it—to work through it once and for all... what then?

Spiritual bypassing is a form of escapism...

What stops us from being our authentic selves is the *'judging'* of others for expressing how they truly feel about what is taking place. When we are judging others for standing in their truth, we are invertedly suppressing our own valid emotions because they feel uncomfortable. We then judge others for being negative or weak in nature and in doing so it may give you a quick fix to your ego by thinking they are not as evolved as you are, only to avoid the adversity that you need to heal.

As already mentioned in a previous chapter Napoleon Hill stated that every adversity, every failure, and every heartache carries with it the seed of an equal or greater benefit. Then why in the hell would we go out of our way to avoid dealing with adversity head-on? When we approach life with a *'good vibes'* only attitude, we are denying our truth, our genuine self—our loyal feelings as if they don't matter. That my friend is damaging, harmful and debilitating beyond any possible physical glitch of evolution!

Spiritual bypassing will keep you in an emotional loop, a pattern of avoidance, repudiation, and denial.. in my experience all that has done is left me from seeking external of myself and going off on a weekend retreat with some enlightened Guru that only makes me feel better temporarily. The minute I return home, I feel anguish all over again.

Spiritual bypassing acts as a cover-up...

Most individuals pretend that everything is okay when really, it's not—and not being present in the here and now, overstating the positive and avoiding the negative aspects of life.

Although spiritual bypassing can be seen as a coping mechanism, it can stifle growth and innovation, stunt your emotional development, and get in your way of unleashing your authentic self!

Psychologist Ingrid Clayton says, *"Spiritual bypass shields us from the truth, it disconnects us from our feelings and helps us avoid the big picture. It is more about checking out than checking in—and the difference is so subtle that we usually don't even know we are doing it."*

Lower vibrational frequencies such as shame, guilt, grief, fear, sadness, and anger will only accumulate. The thing is this, we can only cure our wounds if we attend to them. Imagine not attending to a real wound, what do you think will take place? Your wound would get infected or worse! No wonder there is an increase in stress, anxiety, and depression. When these negative emotions arise, they are telling us that something is not right, maybe our needs are not being met or we have compromised our values or boundaries.

The only pain in pleasure is the pleasure of the pain...

To normalise this concept is to *'accept'* that we all have parts of ourselves that we would rather not look at—from doubts and fears to guilt and shame but when we bury these aspects in our unconscious mind rather than resolve and integrate them, they often take on dysfunctional roles and behaviours that prevent healing and cause harm to ourselves and our relationships! So how do we stop spiritual bypassing for good?

The first step is to get comfortable with being uncomfortable. Life begins at the end of your comfort zone. Yes! We are conditioned to stay in our safe zone. But how are we meant to grow, expand, and succeed if we continue to do what we have always done? If you continue to do what you have always done, you will always get what you have always gotten.

Learning to be a little uncomfortable and be okay with *'not knowing'* is actually very powerful, because, from this vantage point, anything is possible! There are so many benefits to becoming comfortable with being a little uncomfortable. We must exalt ourselves forward and normalise the uncomfortable zone to be able to find our place of productive discomfort.

You must be in it to feel it and step through it as this is where your greatest potential lies. I promise you that you will be extremely surprised, astonished, and dazzled that you will accomplish more than you ever thought was achievable. First of all, see uncomfortable feelings as a sign there is something wrong and something needs to change. Uncomfortable emotions need to be recognised—rather than avoided or masked with superficial positive escapism.

Then, avoid labelling your emotions as *'good'* or *'bad'*. Accept all emotions, recognising that they are temporary – and don't make you a *'bad'* person for having them. Lastly, use negative thoughts and feelings to propel you into positive action. Instead of ignoring them or masking them with an *"it is what it is"* mindset, use them as a catalyst for real change. Ignoring a problem, or sidestepping it, doesn't solve it.

This too shall pass...

So here is an alternative to spiritual bypassing—it's to feel your feelings. All feelings! Live your life knowing and accepting that they are only temporary and that they will eventually pass once you make them feel seen, heard, and valued. And there is nothing wrong with you. We are indeed allowed to have conflicting beliefs, thoughts and feelings about ourselves, our experiences, and the world. All feelings matter, they are valid, and they should not be judged as good or bad but instead have a neutral approach to them.

Acknowledgement is key! We can only work with what is coming up if we accept, recognise, and admit the truth. This of course takes practice, and you know what they say. Practice makes perfect. It's a mindfulness practice. It is a practice of being present in the now, to sit and listen to what is rather than do something about it. And this means allowing others to do the same. We must lead by example. Giving space for others to process their own emotions in the present moment is essential. Have empathy, compassion, and kindness with your bypassing parts.

Dare to face your cognitive dissonance...

Cognitive dissonance appears when an individual's attitude, behaviour, beliefs, ideas, and values do not complement each other or when they hold two contradictory beliefs. It causes a feeling of discomfort that motivates people to try to feel better. People may do this via defence mechanisms, such as avoidance.

Basically, it's when a state of being doesn't align with the behaviours. It's when there is an internal clash, conflict or battle going on. Let's say you want to be healthy, but you don't exercise or eat nutritious food. Or you want to write a book, but you are keeping yourself busy all of the time! You can see that an individual is trying to hold two contradictory beliefs and have a very sophisticated ego. The result of cognitive dissonance is a sense of underlying uneasiness, anxiety, guilt and *"something isn't quite right."*

Those who carry a lot of cognitive dissonances tend to explain the *'why'* they are showing up the way that they are showing up. They give excuses for their behaviour, rather than admitting what is really going on. Cognitive dissonance is another form of spiritual bypassing.

The Law of Acceptance... you are worth it!

Are your receiving channels open? When you declare *"I am open and ready to receive"* the Universe not only hears you, but it also holds out its hands to help you.

There is something called the Universal Law of Giving and Receiving —this means that you can only give what you allow yourself to receive ... and you can only receive what you are willing to give! So, in order to translate that into our human existence, we have to give what we want to receive. If you want happiness, make others happy! If you want love, show it to others. If you want kindness ... put it out there and it will come back to you.

Your greatness is not what you have, it's what you give. Don't expect to receive if you are not willing to give. But ... you know who is going to give you everything in this life? You. Ahem. Yes. And if you are anything like me, this can be a sticking point ... a pain point even.

Sometimes my receiving channels need a bit of clearing, because, like many people, I don't quite know how to receive without feeling guilty. Every time someone pays me a compliment, I always shrug it off or even sometimes downplay it. When I receive a gift, I feel compelled to return the favour in some way. When someone reaches out to me offering a hand ... I kindly reject them with a smile and a thank you— and say, *"it's okay"* (*even if it's not*) because I don't want to bother other people with my stuff.

So, when that is the case, what kind of signs do you think I am sending out to the Universe? Correctamundo!!! '*I am not ready to receive*'. LOUD AND CLEAR. Once I made that realisation, it was quite an '*aha*' moment. I was very quick to change my tone, and believe it or not, this change of mindset has been a miraculous shift, and a miraculous gift.

Life is like a boomerang, what you give is what you get...

Whether we like it or not, our consciousness operates every second of our day. The principle of conscious manifestation is '*acceptance*' – this means accepting the littlest things – like a compliment, allowing someone to help you with your groceries into your car and ... it is about accepting without guilt.

The trick to mastering it is, that you have to become more *'aware'*, so as to be able to stop yourself from talking yourself out of *'acceptance'* because that may just be your saboteur in action! And, you probably don't even know it because you have been doing it for such a long time and wondering why you are still in the same place you were five years ago.

It's about learning to *'surrender'* and *'accept'* all with no judgement. Say what? How do I accept with no judgement? Well, it happens on three levels. The first level is the deepest part of our mind, that greater part of who we are—our unconscious self where all of our beliefs, habits, fears, our unconscious bias, the old programs that no longer serve us – all live in that greater part of our mind. Oh ... and yes, the most important part —what we think and feel about ourselves too.

You are good enough to receive...

So, let's say you have an old mental program that you are not good enough to receive, or not worthy of riches, wealth, health, and abundance. Then guess what? Your judgement or doubt will kick in ... and then, in comes the inner critic—telling you stories like *"they need it more than you"* and *"how can you impose on them"* because blah, blah, blah ... I'm sure you can fill in the blanks.

But hang on a minute. Even after this critic has taken over the show, it doesn't just stop there. There is another layer ... the conditioned mind—the part of us that is *'taught'* by the environment, family, society, and community *"to do this, you need to do that"* and *"this is just the way it is...."* And it's here that we trip ourselves up again because we use this to justify the way things play out in our lives, instead of considering that actually, it is indeed possible to create absolutely anything and everything that we desire. We do things like get married, buy a bigger house, and work our butt off for a promotion because we think that society will approve of us. Sure, we all want approval, but we often seek it without truly following what makes us happy, deep down inside.

It's safe for you to be a powerful human being...

But wait, there's more.... I know. I am sounding like a commercial. The final layer is the conscious aspect of accepting. Once we have silenced our inner critic and worked out that, self-acceptance is more powerful than the opinions of those around us—we can put ourselves in the driver's seat. And this is when the magic happens because we can co-create *'reality'* through our awareness of the benefits of working with unseen energy and frequency. We now know that we have come into this life with a blueprint that influences us, we can use it to our advantage, and we can be inspired to create magnificence for ourselves.

We just have to get out of our own way first. Ditch the lingering doubt and the conditioning, and then what's left is *'acceptance'* and it's bountiful because it provides you with the power to choose—whatever you want, whenever you want. Because when we are consciously accepting, we are consciously manifesting from a place that is much more aligned with our heart and not our mind. Acceptance is the path.

So... The bottom line is to get rid of your own internal negativity and don't base your self-worth on what other people think of you.

Make sure you have your receiving channels open.

- Do you receive compliments well?
- Do you receive unexpected gifts easily?
- Do you accept help when it is offered to you?
- Do you accept your meal being paid for by a friend?

These are little things, but they can provide little signals that will help you know if you are open to receiving them. Remember the Universe is moving through every single one of us, all the time, and it's waiting to support you to create the life you want.

Attract what you want by being what you want...

You are now coming to understand that there is abundance for you, and it is not your job to work out *'how'* it will come to you. However, it is your job to co-create with the Universe—work with everything that comes your way, by *'accepting'* circumstances, events, and incidences. When you get into the flow of your life experience by accepting, you show the Universe that you *'believe'* and that you are ready to receive. And, then once you have done that, the Universe will bring it about—just trust. Remember, the details—how, when, whom etc... are none of your business.

Remember that all we are is a result of what we have thought. Essentially, nothing can come into your experience unless you summon it through persistent thoughts. *"When you believe something is hard, the Universe demonstrates the difficulty. When you believe something is easy, the Universe demonstrates the ease"* eloquently said, Abraham Hicks.

Believing involves thinking, talking, and acting as though you have already received it. Acceptance is about trusting yourself to rise to whatever occasion presents itself to you. It is about being open to ALL of life, knowing that it all has value whether you like it or not. Make sure a *'yes'* to someone else is not a 'no' to yourself.

Asking is the beginning of receiving... The Law of Acceptance is a conscious choice to drop all forms of resistance and make the most of the present moment. Acceptance isn't about liking or approving something. It is about letting life flow and unfold without getting in the way. Remember the other side of giving is receiving... there is value in accepting the situation as it is. And then realising resistance to it doesn't help—and then begin to try and change your attitude, the way you think and feel about it. I promise it will all be worth it.

Non-resistance is the key to bliss, joy, and happiness...

Whenever you feel a level of resistance—that is the first sign that something needs to change. And when you feel *'resistance'* take a good hard look at what are you resisting in the first place. Separate yourself from the resistance because only when you create space between you and the resistance with no judgement you are looking at it from an external point of view rather than being in the resistance. Instead of being head over heels in your sh!t – you are creating distance and when you do it is so much more empowering, it puts you in the driver's seat for you to surrender to the resistance and let go of it.

Resistance is conflicting parts, internal struggles and you fighting against a behavioural change. It's a losing battle so don't waste your time or energy. It takes up way too much brain power, physical, emotional, mental, and spiritual energy to resist such feelings of discomfort. The only way forward is to practice non-resistance. It can be as simple as you trying to control your thoughts, rather than acknowledge them and don't resist them but observe them with non-attachment and non-judgment—just allow your thoughts to come and go like the clouds in a windy sky.

When you let go of the struggle you will experience a deep release that will allow you to find your own truth within. Things will go a lot more smoothly when you surrender control—when you let things happen instead of making them happen. If something feels off to you or something that you can't quite put your finger on it—then don't.

So many of us get it wrong... meaning the moment we get a whiff of something is wrong or there is an untruth that presents itself, we invest our time and energy to find the truth at all costs. We are in fact giving our power away in finding such truth and if anything, pushing it further away from us. Therefore, when you feel such uncertainty don't fish, where you will not find fish but instead go within—find calmness and comfort within and listen to the whispers of your own intuition.

There you will find divinity and magic because your inner wisdom will embrace you and push you towards the light. Your inner wisdom will reinvigorate your creativity and resurrect your spark, your light, and your own truth if you practice non-resistance to what is. Non-resistance is the key to peace.

If there are hidden truths that are not previewed to you—then you must not entertain such illusion but instead stand strong and remain in your centre, be not distracted by external noise and the very thing that feels off to you. In good time it will all be revealed as you are in a non-resistant state of being.

Every thought, every feeling and every action carries with it a frequency. The less you resist—the less the very thing you resist will cease to exist because you have surrendered to what is and thus paying less attention to its presence. Resistance for me often asks me *"what is it that I need to let go of?"* whether that be a belief system or an old repeating narrative that no longer serves me.

This will be different for everyone, it can be letting go of procrastination, self-sabotage or perfectionism which are some of my own resistances that I struggle with on a regular basis.

And this my dearest one is the end of your introduction to the shadow work. I know we have covered a lot of concepts and I truly hope this book has whetted your appetite and left you hungry for more. If you are curious and want to go deeper and do the work, I offer regular workshops and this book is your VIP ticket to discovering more about you.

Go to: The Shadow Workshop
https://shadow.catherineplano.com.au

If there is one thing that I would like to leave you with is to practice non-judgement, non-attachment, and non-resistance because that is the key to true bliss, joy, and happiness. In other words, if you want to become the next Buddha, then you just need to focus on the practice of non-judgement, non-attachment, and non-resistance.

Before I go, if you felt triggered and you are head high in your own sh!t know this my dearest one, it has come up for it to be healed. Give yourself a pat on the shoulder and say, *"well done"*, because you are ready to let go of it all and grab the seeds of wisdom! And know that once you have handled your sh!t, there will be new opportunities for you to apply what you have learned in this book.

Namaste – I appreciate you; I love you and I honour you.

www.ingramcontent.com/pod-product-compliance
Lightning Source LLC
Chambersburg PA
CBHW070729020526
44107CB00077B/2170